· THE BRAVE ESCAPE OF ·

Edith Wharton

⊰ A Biography ⊱

BY CONNIE NORDHIELM WOOLDRIDGE

CLARION BOOKS
HOUGHTON MIFFLIN HARCOURT
BOSTON • NEW YORK • 2010

Clarion Books
215 Park Avenue South, New York, New York 10003
Text copyright © 2010 by Connie Nordhielm Wooldridge

The text was set in 12-point Filosofia.

Quotes from Edith Wharton's published and unpublished works, letters, and journals are
reprinted by permission of the estate of Edith Wharton and the Watkins/Loomis Agency.
Quotes from *Portrait of Edith Wharton* by Percy Lubbock, copyright 1947
by D. Appleton-Century, Inc., used by permission of Dutton, a
division of Penguin Group (USA) Inc.
Quotes from the letters of Ogden Codman, Jr., courtesy of Historic New England.
Quotes from the letters of Henry James used by permission of Bay James for the
estate of Henry James.

For information about permission to reproduce selections from this book, write to
Permissions, Houghton Mifflin Harcourt Publishing Company, 215 Park Avenue South,
New York, New York 10003.

Clarion Books is an imprint of Houghton Mifflin Harcourt Publishing Company.

www.hmhbooks.com

Library of Congress Cataloging-in-Publication Data
Wooldridge, Connie Nordhielm.
The brave escape of Edith Wharton / by Connie Nordhielm Wooldridge.
p. cm.
ISBN 978-0-547-23630-8
1. Wharton, Edith, 1862–1937—Juvenile literature. 2. Authors, American—20th century—
Biography—Juvenile literature. I. Title.

PS3545.H16Z943 2010
813'.52—dc22
[B]   3 1088 1006 6821 7

2009033574
Manufactured in the U.S.A.

DOC 10 9 8 7 6 5 4 3 2 1

4500230684

To Pamela Gail Hartmann,
who wandered across four continents with me
and who always finds a welcome
when she wanders into my thoughts

Edith at her desk at the Mount in 1905, a publicity photo for The House of Mirth.

· CONTENTS ·

1   Different   1

2   Drawing-rooms Are Always Tidy   11

3   Ambition Is a Grievous Fault   24

4   Sunshine in the House   35

5   New Writer Who Counts   52

6   A Republic of the Spirit   67

7   Wych-hazel   88

8   Storm and Sorrow   101

9   The Worst of Doing Good   113

10   I Want to Go Home   131

   Afterword: The Gist of Me   151

   Abbreviations Used in the Notes   154

   Source Notes   156

   Bibliography   168

   Works by Edith Wharton   171

   Picture Credits   174

   Acknowledgments   175

   Index   176

· O N E ·

Different

*There was once a little girl who was so very
intelligent that her parents feared that she would die.*

"The Valley of Childish Things, and Other Emblems,"
short story, 1896

eeping up with the Joneses." This expression was first used
in New York City sometime in the 1800s and is still heard today. "The
Joneses" came to represent wealth and high social status; people who try
to keep up with them are those who badly want to be accepted as upper
class.

Edith Wharton didn't have to worry for a minute about keeping up
with the Joneses. She was one of them. Her mother and father, Lucretia
and George Frederic Jones, were members of the prominent New York
Jones family that inspired the old saying, and so was their daughter,
born Edith Jones. Edith's parents could have told the keeper uppers
that social status had nothing to do with money, though of course the

Joneses had plenty. It had to do with being born into the right family and knowing how to behave properly.

Edith's baptism took place at Grace Church, in New York City, which had society's stamp of approval. Her parents' names were listed in the registry as "George F. & _____" because Lucretia knew a woman's name must appear in print only at her birth, her marriage, and her death. Lucretia Jones was always proper.

Well, maybe not always. Edith's birth, on January 24, 1862, created a bit of a stir because Edith's older brother, Harry, was eleven years old when she was born, and her even older brother, Freddy, was sixteen. New York society didn't ask (that would have been rude), but New York society wondered: Was having a child so late in life entirely proper? Had something unplanned happened? The nursery in their home had long since been put to other use, and their Irish nurse, Hannah Doyle, who without children to tend had become the family seamstress, was hastily called back into service. Lucretia Jones—"*the* Mrs. Jones," she called herself—was perfectly capable of deciding what was proper. So after she gave birth to Edith, she carried on. Properly, of course.

Edith was not affected by the small uproar caused by her arrival into the world. Her childhood memories were sunny ones. When she was around three, she had her portrait painted wearing a beaded necklace and a fancy dress, her red hair parted in the middle and rolled into two tight curls at the top of her head. Her "tall splendid father" was always kind, and his strong arms made her feel safe. Her mother was beautiful and wore gorgeous "flounced dresses." As Edith grew, her two

• • •

Though her family later attended Calvary Episcopal, Edith was baptized at Grace Church (shown here in 1855) because it was more fashionable.

older brothers were "mostly away," but she always had her nurse, Doyley, who was "as established as the sky and as warm as the sun." And she had a small white Spitz puppy named Foxy. She was sure she could communicate with Foxy, and she preferred him to any of her dolls.

Besides her late arrival into the family, there was something else unusual, and potentially improper, about young Edith. The child was alarmingly alert and observant. She appeared to see more than most children saw. When she visited her aunt Elizabeth Jones at her mansion on the Hudson River, Edith decided that her aunt was made of the same steel and granite as the turrets of her grim home. Both Aunt Elizabeth Jones and her house were so ugly, they made Edith miserable and then afraid. Edith was sure there was a wolf under the bed she slept in at Aunt Elizabeth's. After that visit, Edith would drag her nursery stool from room to room in search of Mamma or Doyley whenever she wanted to look at her Red Riding Hood storybook.

Edith's mother began to worry. Surely her daughter's sensitivity and lively imagination didn't make Edith—well—different. There had already been one different member in the family, a rich cousin who spent the last few years of his life sitting on a marble shelf convinced he was a bust of Napoleon. Different was too terrible to think about.

When Edith was four, her father rented out their three-story brownstone house in New York City and their summer home in Newport, Rhode

• • •

Edith's brothers, Freddy (top)
and Harry, around 1856.
Portraits by John Whitten Ehninger.

This portrait of Edith, painted when she was about three (signed "Brady N York"), is the earliest known likeness.

Edith, photographed in England when her family dropped her brother Harry off at Cambridge University.

Island, and took the family on a grand European tour. Edith's oldest brother, Freddy, stayed in New York because he was working on a master's degree at Columbia College. Her second brother, Harry, sailed with them but headed right to Cambridge University as soon as they were across the Atlantic. Edith's nurse, Doyley, was her constant companion. Mr. Jones didn't have a job, because upper-class New York men didn't work for money; they just had it. Since there was no reason to hurry the trip, it ended up lasting six years: a year in Rome, a run through Spain, two years in Paris, a visit to Germany, and a two-year stay in Florence.

Edith was dazzled by Europe. It was full of breathtaking scenery and buildings that seemed to have been around since the beginning of time. There was something established and good about the oldness of Europe. She took in every bit of it—the sights, the smells, the sounds—and stored it all away in the very warmest part of her young heart. New York faded from her memory. It was Europe she thought of as home.

When Edith was six, the Jones family settled in Paris, on the Right Bank of the Seine River, for two years. Edith learned to speak French, and two new worlds opened up for her. The first was the world of "making up." She had always imagined tales and stories, but she didn't want to tell them, she wanted to read them aloud from a book. The fact that she hadn't learned to read yet didn't slow her down for a minute. She would seize a book (and it had to be a particular kind of book with thick black print), shut herself in her mother's room, pace up and down the floor holding the book open (sometimes upside down), and "read" her invented story out loud, turning the pages as the twists and turns of the plot poured out of her imagination. When the urge to make up a story came, she had to obey. If the urge came while she was playing with a nice child who had been invited to visit for the day, she would bolt from the room, find her mother, and announce, "Mamma, you must go and entertain that little girl for me. *I've got to make up.*"

A portrait of Edith's father, George Frederic Jones, around the time of his marriage in 1844, by John Whitten Ehninger.

Her mother was both fascinated and alarmed. This making-up business was yet another worrying sign that Edith might be different. At the same time, Lucretia was dying to hear the stories Edith was creating. Not wanting to interrupt the mysterious process occurring on the other side of the door to her own bedroom, Lucretia pressed her ear against the keyhole and tried to write down what she heard. But her daughter's words came more quickly than Lucretia's pen could move, so she gave up.

The second of Edith's new worlds opened when her father, who had studied literature at college, decided it was time for his daughter to learn to read. He had a plan. First he would teach Edith the alphabet. Then he would teach her short words like "cat" and "bat." Before George Frederic had proceeded too far with his plan, he and Lucretia discovered their daughter sitting under a table in the drawing room, absolutely motionless, with a book in her lap.

They asked her what she was doing.

"Reading," she answered.

Her disbelieving parents asked her to read aloud and determined, to their surprise, that Edith could, in fact, read. This threw them into a

. . .

*Lucretia Jones loved beautiful clothes, and Edith always
wanted to look as pretty as her mother.*

panic, probably because the book Edith had picked for her first try was
a play about a prostitute.

In Lucretia's view, books could be dangerous. Not only were they
full of bad people, they were full of bad English. Especially children's
books. Louisa May Alcott was so sloppy with her grammar in *Little*

Women that Lucretia was appalled. A few children's books—such as George MacDonald's *The Princess and the Goblin* and Charles Kingsley's *The Water-Babies*—met Lucretia's standard. But adult books were grammatically more correct and therefore safer. So from that time on, Edith was permitted to read only adult classics approved by her mother. And until she was safely married off, the reading of contemporary novels was strictly forbidden. Novels were full of situations no young girl should be exposed to.

Edith promptly began devouring adult classics. That created even more worries for her mother. It was believed at the time that a young lady could destroy her health by learning too much. Even worse, what if all this reading meant Edith was intelligent? Nothing was harder than to marry off an intelligent daughter.

Edith was too young to appreciate the danger she was in, so she kept reading. If her young mind couldn't make sense of all the grown-up thoughts she bumped into, she just enjoyed the sound of the words. When Grandmother Rhinelander, Lucretia's mother, came to Paris to visit, reading became Edith's way of communicating with her. Grandmamma was quite deaf, and modern hearing aids had not yet been invented. She relied on a trumpet-shaped device, holding the small end close to her ear so that the bell-shaped end would pick up some of the sounds her ears missed. As soon as Edith appeared, Grandmamma would lay aside her needlework and pick up her ear trumpet. To Edith, that meant this wonderful, ancient woman was waiting for words. And what better place to get words than books? So Edith would find a book of poems in her father's library (the poetry of Alfred, Lord Tennyson, was a favorite), and for hours she would shout poems, one after the other, into her grandmother's ear trumpet.

Memories of a Paris dance class with Mademoiselle Michelet when she was six or seven were not so pleasant. She could get through the dancing, though it wasn't one of her stronger skills. The sight of

Mademoiselle's "small shrivelled bearded mother" at the piano, how-ever, she could not endure. Mademoiselle Michelet's mother was as ugly as her aunt Elizabeth Jones, and Edith felt disgusted and afraid all over again. Edith whispered to a little boy in the class that Mademoi-selle's mother looked like *"une vieille chèvre"* (an old goat).

Immediately she was overcome with guilt. She had said something *"about* Mlle. Michelet's mother" that she "would not have said *to* her." Lucretia would certainly not approve. Good girls didn't talk behind peo-ple's backs. Edith felt she had to atone for her naughtiness. She gath-ered her courage and, with no prompting beyond her own severe conscience, confessed her whispered comment in front of the entire dance class. The reward for her honesty was a stern scolding from Mademoiselle for being impertinent. It wasn't the last time Edith would feel compelled to speak a truth no one thought should be told, nor would it be the last time she would be rebuked for it.

In Paris, Mr. Henry Bedlow, a gentleman friend of the family's, often visited on Sundays. Children of well-to-do families didn't dine with the adults, so Edith was always "led in with the dessert," her long red hair rolled into sausage-shaped curls. She was allowed to sit on their visitor's lap. Instead of fairy tales, which didn't interest Edith, this friend told her fascinating stories from Greek mythology. Edith lived in a world full of adults, and she was suspicious of stories that were made up especially for children. But the myths about the gods and goddesses who lived on Mount Olympus, their domestic jealousies and spats, were different. These stories were a large version of the dramas Edith had begun to notice in her parents' real world. It was real life that Edith wanted to know about.

In the summer of 1870, when Edith was eight years old, war broke out between France and Prussia. This war would end unhappily for France, so it was fortunate that, just before it erupted, the Jones family left Paris for a spa in the Black Forest of Germany. There Edith studied the German language, and there she almost died of typhoid fever. But this black cloud in her life had a silver lining: When she was recovering, her parents set aside their worry that she was becoming "bookish" and let her read everything they could find, as long as it met their strict standards.

The Joneses' European tour ended with a two-year stay in Florence, Italy. Her parents gave Edith a new puppy, Florentine Foxy, to replace the Foxy she'd had to leave in New York. And a charming young lady taught her yet another language: Italian. The family's suite in Florence was perfect for "making up." Folding doors linked one room to another creating a "matchless track" for her "sport." She would wait for the grownups to go out and for Doyley to pick up her sewing. Then she would seize a book and pace through the suite, "pouring forth undisturbed" a "tireless torrent" of stories. The fact that she could actually read only seemed to feed her passion.

· · ·

Edith at age eight, after her battle with typhoid fever.

It was 1872 when ten-year-old Edith and her family boarded a ship that would take them back to New York City. She could speak French, German, and Italian. She was wealthy, privileged, and envied by those who wanted to keep up with the Joneses. And she had no idea that she was any of those things. While she was traveling the world, her entire small world—her parents and Doyley—had traveled with her, like a cast of actors moving together from one stage to another. They socialized not with Europeans but with other wealthy Americans on their own grand tours.

Freddy was married and waiting for the family in New York, where he now lived with his wife, Minnie, and new baby daughter, Beatrix. Although he hadn't been with the family in Europe for more than brief visits, he and his wife were perfect examples of the life Edith would be expected to live. Edith Jones should marry a wealthy man who could provide her with dresses and jewelry. She should mind her manners and keep company with people of birth, background, and breeding who knew how to mind theirs. She should pay attention to a governess, who would soon be hired to teach Edith just what she needed to know and nothing more.

As it turned out, Lucretia was right to be concerned that her daughter was different and, even worse, intelligent. Edith Jones looked like a perfectly innocent ten-year-old as she steamed across the Atlantic bound for a home she didn't really know. But Edith's keen eye, her reading, her making up, and her need to tell the truth were the beginnings of her brave escape from the expectations of the society into which she'd been born.

TWO

Drawing-rooms Are Always Tidy

*All talents are not developped [sic] at once, but lie
dormant until some magic touch awakens them.*

Fast and Loose, *1876–77*

The Civil War had been over for six years by the time the Joneses' ship brought them home to New York City. In 1872 a new war was raging. It was a class war between Old New York society (the "nobs") and the new-money people (the "swells"), between the aristocratic Joneses and those trying to use their money to keep up with them.

New York City had boomed while the Jones family was away. The number of factories almost doubled, new industries sprang up, and nobodies suddenly became millionaires. That was fine, until the newly rich nobodies tried, as one Jones relative put it, to "climb boldly over the walls of social exclusiveness." That meant war, and Caroline Astor, Edith's first cousin once removed, sprang to the defense of the Old Guard.

Ward McAllister, shown here in a photograph from 1876, was obsessed by such social details as the wording of an invitation or the color of a sheet of note paper.

Caroline Astor, photographed in 1875, entertained hundreds of guests each year in her three houses. When a self-made millionaire named Alexander Stewart built a mansion across from hers at Fifth Avenue and Thirty-fourth Street, she saw it as a challenge to her social authority and refused to invite him to any of her events.

The year Edith's family returned from Europe, Mrs. Astor teamed up with Ward McAllister, who was a nobody himself, but at least he was fighting on the right side. They created a group called the Patriarchs: twenty-five carefully selected men who gave three exclusive balls each year. A Patriarch could invite four ladies and five gentlemen to each ball, but he had to be sure his guests were acceptable. Swells could be invited, but only after they had proved they knew how to dress, how to behave, and whose company to be seen in. To a swell, attending one of the Patriarchs' Balls meant being well on the way to the Promised Land of high society.

In opening the gates to even a few of these "climbers," the members of the Old Guard began to look more and more like those they were defending themselves against. Old-fashioned, tasteful private gatherings began to give way to showy, public social events. Responsible, careful spending was replaced by tasteless displays of wealth. Women ordered gowns from Paris that cost $2,500 each ($42,000 in today's dollars). One woman threw an expensive party for her friends' dogs. Mrs. Astor herself had so many jewels that she wore one diamond necklace in front and another hanging down her back.

None of this escaped Edith's alert young eyes. Years later, she would write about "all the strange weeds pushing up between the ordered rows of social vegetables." In her stories neither the "weeds" nor the "vegetables" came out looking particularly good. It was the truth that mattered to her.

Lucretia and the rest of the family could be forgiven for not noticing that Edith was observing all of this. In fact, Edith appeared refreshingly like a proper child upon their arrival stateside. Since it was June, the Joneses were soon out of New York and off to Pencraig, the family's summer home in Newport, Rhode Island. Edith had no memories of Pencraig from before the trip to Europe, and it was like a brand-new place to her. All of a sudden she could be a child again. "To a little girl long pent up in hotels and flats there was inexhaustible delight in the freedom of a staircase to run up and down, of lawns and trees, a meadow full of clover and daisies, a pony to ride, terriers to romp with," a private beach, and a dock.

The whole family was in Newport together for the summer. Harry, whom Edith adored, had finished college in England and was home, about to propose to a young woman who lived nearby. And Freddy, whom Edith didn't like half as well, had left New York for the summer and moved into Pencraig Cottage, a small house on the family property, with his wife and baby daughter.

Freddy's wife, Minnie, spoke French fluently and had all the characteristics of a perfect society lady. But she was unusual in that she preferred intelligent conversation to social babble. Of course, this drew Edith to her immediately. Minnie was equally struck by her clever young sister-in-law. And what could be more wonderful than Freddy and Minnie's newborn baby, Beatrix. Minnie and Beatrix made it easier to put up with Freddy.

Right next door to the Newport summer home of George Frederic Jones was the home of Lewis Rutherford and his family. "There was

• • •

Pencraig, the summer home of the Jones family in Newport, Rhode Island.

certainly a continual coming and going through the private gate between the properties," Edith recalled. Professor Rutherford's two grown daughters, Margaret and Louisa, were goddesses to Edith—just like the ones in the myths she'd heard in Paris. There were also two Rutherford boys close to Edith's age. Before very long she had a violent crush on the one named Winthrop.

Because Margaret and Louisa Rutherford were "out"—old enough to officially take part in adult society—their German governess, Anna Bahlmann, was no longer needed. She came to work for the Joneses. Anna introduced her young charge to German literature, and Edith later claimed that without this governess, her "mind would have starved at the age when the mental muscles are most in need of feeding."

The best thing about Newport was the weekly walk Professor Rutherford led over a rugged country path called the Rocks. "Every Sunday," Edith remembered, "he used to collect the children of the few friends living near us, and take them, with his own, for a tramp across this rugged country to the sea. Yet what I recall of those rambles is not so much the comradeship of the other children, or the wise and friendly talk of our guide, as my secret sensitiveness to the landscape . . . to every detail of wind-warped fern and wide-eyed briar rose." It seemed to Edith that there was a "unifying magic" behind the scenery and that she was "in deep and solitary communion" with nature in a way the other children weren't. Family summers in Newport—that first one and the eight that followed—were pure joy.

When the summer season was over, it was back to New York City, or, more exactly, to the Jones part of the city. The homes of the Jones clan were scattered about near Fifth Avenue starting at Eighth Street to the south and running north to Edith's house on West Twenty-third. Before Edith was born, her ancient aunt Mary Mason had pushed the family territory all the way to Fifty-eighth Street by building a house there. At the time, the family members were shocked. They weren't sure they could safely travel that far uptown—almost into the country. Then they slowly got used to the idea, and the boundaries of their tiny New York world expanded ever so slightly.

As Edith remembered it, New York was full of rows and rows of

• • •

New York society parading along Fifth Avenue on a Sunday afternoon after church, painted in the late 1800s by American impressionist Childe Hassam.

houses, built out of "the most hideous stone ever quarried." The Joneses' brownstone was as ugly as all the others on the block. And the inside, suffocated by draperies and crowded with heavy furniture, was as ugly as the outside. After the beauty of Europe, New York City—even the high-class Jones part—was a terrible letdown.

A formal photograph of fourteen-year-old Edith. When she became famous, as an adult, her shyness was often mistaken for arrogance.

But in the brownstone where Edith lived was her father's library, and George Frederic invited ten-year-old Edith to wander into it anytime she wanted to. She spent hours there. "No children of my own age, and none even among the nearest of my grown-ups, were as close to me as the great voices that spoke to me from books," Edith recalled. Plutarch's history, Homer's and Milton's epics, and Keats's poetry were all within her reach. She would squat down "on the thick Turkey rug, pulling open one after another the glass doors of the low bookcases, and dragging out book after book." She kept her book adventures in her father's library to herself, never breathing a word about them to anyone.

It was also in her father's library that Edith did her writing. And when she wrote, she was entering dangerous territory. Her father and his friends "held literature in great esteem," and every gentleman had a library full of good books. But New York society "stood in nervous dread of those who produced" that literature. Poets were socially acceptable, but novelists and newspaper writers were to be avoided at all cost. As far as Old New York was concerned, writing was "something between a black art and a form of manual labour."

Edith was not a writer, she was a child playing at writing, so her parents humored her. They didn't go so far as to provide her with paper on which to scratch out her poems and stories, but they looked the other way when she claimed the large sheets of wrapping paper from the parcels delivered to the Joneses' home. Edith made it clear to the servants that these sheets were hers. She dragged them to her room and kept stacks ready to be written on. It didn't occur to her to cut the sheets into pages. When she wrote, she spread the papers on the floor and crawled on her hands and knees, filling them up in columns.

In 1873, when she was eleven, Edith decided to write a novel. It began:

> "Oh, how do you do, Mrs. Brown?" said Mrs. Tompkins.
> "If only I had known you were going to call I should have tidied up the drawing-room."

Then she shyly let her mother read her opening lines. Lucretia returned them with the comment: "Drawing-rooms are always tidy."

Edith knew full well that drawing rooms were not always tidy. Things got out of place when guests weren't there. Her parents behaved differently when company wasn't around. But her mother's criticism was more than she could bear. Edith decided to leave off novel writing for a time and turn to poetry, which was more socially acceptable.

When Edith was thirteen, she met the girl who became the most cherished friend of her youth, Emelyn Washburn. Emelyn was nineteen, and her father was Dr. Edward Washburn, the rector of Calvary Episcopal Church, where the Joneses now attended services. Emelyn recognized immediately that Edith was "starving for mental nourishment." The two sat together in church every week. Edith got so swept up in Dr. Washburn's reading from the King James Bible that she unconsciously began pulling the hairs out of Emelyn's camel-hair coat, one by one. To protect her coat, Emelyn gave her friend a pearl button on a string that she could quietly pull back and forth as she listened.

Lucretia and George Frederic Jones led a quiet, refined life in New York City centered around family, social, and church activities. Edith's days followed a set routine. She prepared her lessons in the morning while Doyley brushed her hair. Then came lessons with her governess, Anna Bahlmann. In the afternoons she could ride around with her mother in her carriage or go with her father to whatever might be happening at church. Or Doyley might take her to visit the Washburns. Edith could explore Dr. Washburn's library and write notes (which were never sent) to Winthrop Rutherford on a new contraption of Dr. Washburn's called a typewriter. Sometimes Edith and her friend would climb out Emelyn's window onto the roof, where they would sit and read Dante aloud to each other.

From Emelyn, Edith heard about a part of New York that was as far away from the sheltered Jones blocks as the moon. Emelyn's New York, for example, included the Italians who lived on Mulberry Street. Emelyn had poor vision and thought that riding ferries and watching the scenery might be good for her, so she took frequent trips across the East River and back, watching the gulls and talking to deck hands. Edith was always accompanied by an adult when she went out, and she knew only the good old families of the city, which didn't include deck hands. Emelyn's reading boundaries also stretched further than Edith's. Emelyn was allowed to read the works of the German poet Goethe, who was considered irreligious. Somehow Emelyn managed to convince Lucretia to let Edith read him as well.

As Edith entered adolescence, she became self-conscious and painfully shy. She decided that she was the least attractive member of the family. She thought her hands and feet were too large, because her

brothers were always teasing her about them. She could forgive Harry, whose life had taken a tragic turn when the ship carrying his fiancée to Paris had sunk and she and her family were drowned. But Freddy's teasing stung, and he had wonderful Minnie for a wife, so there was no excuse for him.

To add to her adolescent misery, her mother criticized her for using long words and for not having as much heart as her brothers. Edith's secret worlds of reading and imagining, and the way she seemed to step back and watch what was going on around her, made her appear distant.

And then there were the confusing feelings she had when she was around boys. She described them as "ringing in my ears, humming in my blood, flushing my cheeks & waving in my hair." What were these feelings, she asked her mother. She was too young to understand, she was told. There was no such thing as sex education in the 1870s. Society women were expected to keep their daughters completely shielded from the subject of sex and hope they would miraculously know what to do on their wedding night. Lucretia Jones took seriously this responsibility to shield Edith from anything as crude as the subject of sex.

When she was very young, an older cousin had shocked Edith with the news that babies came from people and not from flowers. Back then, Edith had worked out her own theory on just how that happened: Babies must be born because God looked through the roof of the church and saw a man and a woman getting married. But Edith was curious, and now that she was older, she was aware that something was wrong with her theory, that there was something people weren't telling her. So she turned to her governess. Edith had heard about the passion of love. What was it, she asked Anna. "Why, my dear, there's *nothing* in it," Anna told her. "All my married friends tell me so." Edith didn't believe that for a minute. She was certain there was something in it. She'd secretly read novels about men and women having feelings for one another.

Just before her fifteenth birthday, she started writing another novel. She had gotten hold of a 6½-by-8½-inch notebook, and when it was completed, her story filled 119 of its pages. She titled it *Fast and Loose,* and on the title page she used a male pseudonym, David Olivieri, probably because women novelists were considered socially unacceptable.

Her story began with a quote from *Lucile,* one of the novels she'd promised her mother she wouldn't read:

> Let woman beware
> How she plays fast & loose thus with human despair
> And the storm in man's heart.

The 30,000-word story that followed was a lively romance, full of humor and tragedy, in which the young heroine, Georgina, rejects her true love, marries a wealthy older man, and winds up miserable.

Even as a young writer of fifteen, Edith knew instinctively that a first draft needed to be polished. So she made corrections. In her novel, Georgina's rejected lover goes completely downhill in the short space of two months. Edith fiddled with the dates but just couldn't figure out how to give her hero the proper amount of time to ruin his life.

She had grown wiser since her first writing attempt when she was eleven. *Fast and Loose* would have been frowned upon by proper adults like her mother. So no proper adults were given the chance to read it. She showed it only to Emelyn. Edith also wrote her own mock reviews as if they had actually appeared in the *Saturday Review of Literature*, the *Pall Mall Budget*, and the *Nation*. In her role as critic, she

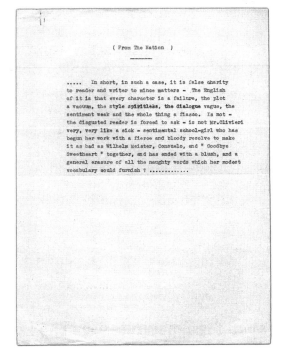

One of Edith's mock reviews of her first novel. She wrote it longhand, then typed it. This was her writing routine for the rest of her life.

completely trashed her own novel: A "twaddling romance," Edith-the-reviewer wrote about Edith-the-author's book; "a chaos of names apparently all seeking their owners," Edith-the-reviewer continued. And then (in case the reader had somehow missed the point), "every character is a failure, the plot a vacuum, the style spiritless, the dialogue vague, the sentiments weak, & the whole thing a fiasco." Perhaps by making light of her own work, Edith was trying to lessen the sting of anything negative Emelyn, her only reader, might say.

Fortunately, Emelyn was all encouragement. She loved *Fast and Loose.* She loved the plot and the style and especially the "reviews." In sharing this work with her friend, Edith was confessing the great sin she had kept locked inside her: She was not just playing at writing. She wanted to be a writer. She wanted to be a writer of the worst kind, a novelist. Emelyn suggested that translating a German poem might be a good writer's exercise. When Edith had finished this assignment, Dr. Washburn read it and thought it was good enough to send off to a magazine. It was accepted and published, but not with Edith's name on it. It wasn't her birth, her marriage, or her death, so it wouldn't have been proper for her name to appear in print. Dr. Washburn signed his name to the piece and presented Edith with the fifty-dollar check he received—her very first earnings as a writer.

Lucretia, of course, knew nothing of her daughter's novel writing. But she kept a notebook of Edith's poems. Just before Christmas of 1878, when Edith was sixteen, her mother arranged to have two dozen of the poems privately published. The small book called *Verses* was circulated to friends and family. Even though everyone knew who the writer was, the poems were unsigned. But Edith's own copy proudly proclaimed:

> Who wrote these verses, she this volume owns.
> Her unpoetic name is Edith Jones.

Her brother Harry showed the poems to a Newport neighbor and editor of the *North American Review*, Allen Thorndike Rice, who sent copies of several of them to his writer friend Henry Wadsworth Longfellow. Longfellow sent them to *his* friend William Dean Howells, the editor of the *Atlantic Monthly*. Mr. Howells was impressed. And so it was that in 1880, five of Edith's poems appeared in one of the most respected literary magazines of the day—anonymously, of course.

There was hardly time for Edith to feel proud of this accomplishment before her poet's hopes were dashed by Allen Thorndike Rice, the Newport neighbor who had been so impressed by *Verses*. Mr. Rice didn't think short poems would get Edith much of anywhere. "What you want to do is to write an epic," he told her. "All the great poets have written epics. Homer . . . Milton . . . Byron. Why don't you try your hand . . . ?"

Write an epic? Like the ones in her father's library? It was too much for Edith to even consider. Way too much. She "shrank" back into her "secret retreat." She was convinced she was "unfitted to be either a poet or a novelist."

It would be a long time before her next publication. Whatever writing Edith did over the next nine years would be kept safely hidden away.

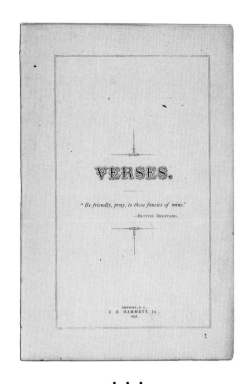

The title page of Edith's poetry collection, published anonymously.

THREE

Ambition Is a Grievous Fault

*Nothing in life need be faced and fought out while
one could pay for a passage to Europe!*

The Fruit of the Tree, *1907*

*I*t was becoming uncomfortably clear to Lucretia Jones that her daughter, Edith, was, in fact, different. Edith did love clothes. That was a relief. That was normal. But Edith's other world of books and ideas was pulling her in a direction Lucretia found mysterious and unsettling. One of the fictional characters Edith later created would describe the "universe of thought" as an "enchanted region which, to those who have lingered there, comes to have so much more colour and substance." Lucretia never "lingered" in that particular "enchanted region," and she certainly didn't think it was a good place for her daughter to be lingering.

Edith needed to understand that her future lay in proper New York society life, her mother thought. The way into that life was to marry a man of birth, background, and breeding. And it was certainly *hoped* that he would have money, though of course that couldn't be stated out loud.

The way to find such a man was to begin attending the Patriarchs' Balls under the watchful eyes of Caroline Astor, now the acknowledged queen of society, and Ward McAllister, known in the press as "The Lord High Separator of the Sheep from the Goats." The way to find such a man was to be seen at the opera and other proper social gatherings. And the way for a young woman's family to let the social world know their daughter was ready to be included in these events was to

· · ·

Edith (standing) with two unidentified people, possibly her mother, Lucretia, and her brother Harry.

throw a coming-out party for her. The usual coming-out age was eighteen, but seventeen-year-old Edith's situation was looking so desperate that Lucretia decided to overlook that rule. Edith spent too much time reading, so she would come out a year early.

At least, that's what Edith was told. But Lucretia shared with Emelyn Washburn the real reasons for the rush to get Edith "out" into society. Mr. Jones's health was going downhill. One of the reasons for his decline was the family's financial situation. Mr. Jones had made some poor investments, and his inherited fortune was dwindling away. Their six-year trip to Europe when Edith was a child had not been an extravagance but a necessity. Renting out their two houses had provided the family with some much-needed money.

• • •

The Academy of Music opened its doors in 1854. By 1878, attending the opera at the academy was a must for New York society. Mrs. Astor often arrived during the second act and left before the finale because she didn't like death scenes.

No matter how far down her nose Mrs. Jones looked at the social upstarts, they had money, and the Joneses, increasingly, did not. In fact, the Joneses were struggling to keep up appearances. Their house on West Twenty-third Street was mortgaged and might have to be sold. Edith's marriage prospects would vanish as soon as it was apparent that the family money was running out. What her mother wanted for Edith was one New York–Newport social season and a marriage proposal from a proper young man.

Edith's coming out would not be one of the tasteless public affairs at Delmonico's Restaurant, which were then the rage with the new-money set. Lucretia's daughter "could meet all the people she need know without being advertised." Edith's debut would take place in the ballroom of the private mansion of a family friend, Mrs. Levi Morton, who was a woman of old wealth and European connections and one of the few, besides Caroline Astor, who even had a ballroom.

On her big night late in 1879, Edith made her appearance in a low-cut gown with a pale green bodice and a ruffled white skirt. Her dress left her shoulders bare for the first time in her life. Her angular features, long nose, and square jaw gave her a serious, severe look. Her red-gold hair was piled on top of her head, and she carried a bouquet of lilies of the valley sent by a friend. She was terrified. As opinionated and confident as she appeared to those close to her, she hated being looked at by a roomful of eyes. She described the beginning of her coming-out evening as "a long cold agony of shyness." But Harry's friends asked her to dance, and then a string of young men her own age lined up to do the same, and her night turned into "a pink blur of emotion." All her dancing partners seemed to like her. Everyone wanted to talk to her. Edith was shocked, relieved, pleased.

Edith went on to have the one social season Lucretia so desperately wanted for her. Harry was well liked, and Edith simply rode to popularity on his coattails. She met friends at the opera on Mondays and Fridays. She was invited to fancy dress balls where she danced into the wee hours of the morning. "For the rest of the winter, I don't think I missed a ball; & wherever I went I had all the dancers I wanted," she remembered. "I tasted all the sweets of popularity. . . . I led, I dominated, I was conscious of 'counting' wherever I went." She spent time with various Jones and Rhinelander cousins and with the Astors. She also socialized with the new-money Vanderbilts. Edith Jones and high society danced their way through the winter and spring in New York, then gathered to picnic and sail at Newport, Rhode Island.

Some found Edith's aristocratic manner and her unexpected bursts of bookish talk hard to take. But a young man named Henry Stevens (known as Harry) thought everything about Edith Jones was charming and fell hopelessly in love with her. He pursued Edith through the New York season. When the social scene shifted to Newport, boating, and the brand-new game of lawn tennis, he continued his pursuit. He was handsome and popular, and he loved organizing social outings and playing games.

In fact, Harry looked like just the man Lucretia Jones was seeking for her daughter. But there was a problem: Harry Stevens was the son of Mrs. Paran Stevens, who was herself the daughter of a grocer. Harry's father's pedigree had been just as bad. He had begun his career with a job in a kitchen and had worked his way up from there. When Harry's father died, he left Mrs. Stevens and Harry a tidy fortune, which Mrs. Stevens used to buy a fashionable house in New York. From this beach-head, she hammered away at Old New York society until a member of the Old Guard called on her at home. This was the stamp of approval Mrs. Stevens had been waiting for. It was all too much for Edith's mother. Mrs. Stevens might have money, but she was lacking in birth, breeding, and background. She simply did not belong, and Mrs. Jones (in polite, tasteful ways, of course) let Mrs. Paran Stevens know that.

Harry, however, was smitten with Edith and fiercely determined. Newport society began to wonder if Harry Stevens and Edith Jones were secretly engaged. "I don't think so," Edith's Newport neighbor Louisa Rutherford wrote to her older sister, Margaret, who was now married and living in Paris. "But appearances are against me, as they are together perpetually when they walk or drive, and Stevens is her shadow."

Late in July 1880, the Jones and Rutherford families migrated north to Bar Harbor, a fashionable resort town on an island off the coast of Maine where Freddy and Minnie Jones were building a cottage. Harry Stevens followed, and society's gossip mill cranked into overdrive: Surely, surely the two must be engaged. Louisa Rutherford kept her sister, Margaret, informed: Edith "still smiles on the attentions of Mr. S.," she wrote. "But I can't believe she means to marry him."

· · ·

Harry Stevens reportedly brought the brand-new game of lawn tennis to Newport, where it replaced archery as society's favorite sport.

Harry wasn't the only one paying attention to Edith. All the young men seemed attracted to her. Louisa was content to have Edith look on her and her sister as goddesses, but when Edith herself attracted a following, Louisa jealously hinted to her sister that Edith let young men "take liberties" with her.

Louisa Rutherford would not have to endure a second social season in the shadow of Edith's popularity. By late fall 1880, George Frederic Jones's health was markedly worse. Only fifty-eight years old, he had sunken cheeks and was constantly nervous and irritable. His doctors prescribed the usual cure for the wealthy: an extended trip to someplace warm. So in November, the Joneses headed for the French Riviera via London and Venice.

A normal eighteen-year-old debutante as popular as Edith would probably have had to be dragged away from the New York–Newport social scene. But Edith Jones was an unusual eighteen-year-old. She had been dreaming of returning to Europe ever since she'd left it at the age of ten. "What were society and dancing and

. . .

Edith in a casual yachting or sporting outfit,
just after her return to Europe.

tennis compared to the rapture of seeing again all that, for eight years, my eyes had pined for?" she wrote. She made her second voyage to Europe "without a backward glance! . . . From that day I never had a pang of regret for 'society'—I was drunk with seeing & learning!"

Edith was so happy to be back in Europe, she seemed not to realize how serious her father's condition was. In the spring of 1881, she heard that Emelyn Washburn had lost her father to a stroke, and she sent her old friend some verses to comfort her. But she never suspected that her own father was close to death. "I became accustomed to his patient inactivity, and probably thought of him as old rather than ill," she wrote.

Harry Stevens caught up with the Joneses in Venice and followed them to Cannes on the Riviera in early 1882. He was so supportive and so obviously devoted to Edith that Lucretia began to warm up to him. She confessed, in a letter to Emelyn, that she found his company a comfort. Harry was with them when Mr. Jones suffered a stroke and became paralyzed. Harry was still there when Mr. Jones died in March 1882.

Edith was at her father's bedside. Many years later, she wrote, "I am still haunted by the look in his dear blue eyes, which had followed me so tenderly for nineteen years, and now tried to convey the goodbye messages he could not speak." Edith felt her father shared her love of books and ideas. But he had dutifully played the part his wife and society expected of him. As he was laid to rest in Cannes, Edith sensed that he was "haunted by something always unexpressed and unattained." What might her father have been if his choices had been braver?

. . .

George Frederic Jones in 1881,
a year before his death.

Edith and her mother and, of course, Harry Stevens returned to the United States a few weeks later. Lucretia's life was completely changed by her husband's death. She never again lived in the family home on West Twenty-third Street, though she kept it as a rental property. And she never returned to Calvary Church, which had now lost both her husband and the rector, Dr. Washburn. She gave up entertaining, and she stopped attending social events. She kept Pencraig, her Newport home, but it was no longer filled with people each summer as it once had been.

There were bright spots, however, even in that dark time. Lucretia inherited a large piece of family property, which put an end to her financial worries. She purchased a home in New York on West Twenty-fifth Street, which was nearer to Freddy and Minnie and their ten-year-old daughter, Beatrix. Freddy was close to his mother and visited her every day. And little Beatrix adored her grandmother.

It looked as if Lucretia had finally succeeded in marrying Edith off. On August 19, 1882, a New York City gossip magazine called *Town Topics: The Journal of Society* announced that "Mr. Henry Stevens, only son of Mrs. Paran Stevens, is reported to be engaged to Miss Edith Jones, daughter of the late George F. Jones, Esq." It might have been Mrs. Stevens who ran the announcement. She loved having her name in print. But Mrs. Stevens certainly wasn't acting as if she were about to become a mother-in-law. Society expected her to host an event celebrating the coming wedding. She didn't.

Unlike her son, Mrs. Stevens was not well liked. Emelyn Washburn, who knew her from Calvary Church, thought the woman would be an "impossible mother-in-law." So it could have been either her difficult personality or her questionable background that kept her from doing the proper thing. It turned out to be much more serious than that. It soon became obvious that Harry's mother was determined to undo the engagement. Within two months, she had succeeded: On October 28, 1882, *Town Topics* reported that "the marriage of Mr. Henry Stevens,

Mrs. Paran Stevens's son, to Miss Edith Jones, which was announced for the latter part of this month, has been postponed, it is said, indefinitely." That was the newspaper's polite way of saying the engagement had been broken.

New York society immediately set about gossiping its way to the exact reason for the break. Did Mrs. Stevens's social wounds run so deep that she would sacrifice her son's happiness to avenge them? One of Edith's Rhinelander cousins thought so. She insisted that "Mrs. S behaved insultingly to Aunt Lu! . . . Mrs. S is at the bottom of it all." Years later, someone described Mrs. Stevens as "an ambitious woman, eager for social prestige, [who] stamped out everything that stood in the pathway of her ambition."

Or was it money? Her late husband's fortune was her ticket into society. If Harry married, most of that fortune would be his. Did she break up the engagement to keep her hands on the money promised to Harry?

The *Newport Daily News* (undoubtedly quoting Mrs. Stevens) had a different angle: "The only reason assigned for the breaking of the engagement hitherto existing between Harry Stevens and Miss Edith Jones is an alleged preponderance of intellectuality on the part of the intended bride. Miss Jones is an ambitious authoress, and it is said that, in the eyes of Mr. Stevens, ambition is a grievous fault."

Whatever the real reason for the break, it was the newspaper's story that took hold. Edith was obviously nowhere near as fond of Harry Stevens as he was of her, so her heart would probably have recovered quickly. But this revealing of her defects in print was completely devastating: She was intellectual, she was ambitious, she wanted to be an authoress. In the scrupulously honest depths of her soul, Edith knew that each charge was absolutely true.

Lucretia Jones wasn't about to put up with any accusing stares or wagging tongues. She booked passage on a steamer and fled, with Edith, to Paris. They returned to New York a few months later, in time for the

• • •

A romantic picture of Edith in the snow, taken in New York in the 1880s.

second Patriarchs' Ball of the season. It was held at Delmonico's, which Lucretia and the rest of society's Old Guard had grudgingly learned to tolerate. Edith's invitation to this particular ball was a clear signal: Society had been gracious. Society forgave her trespass of putting her literary dreams above her duty to marry. As she walked into Delmonico's, Edith trembled and clutched the arm of her escort. It was as if she were coming out all over again. She faced the event bravely, but now all she wanted was to make it through the evening with her dignity intact.

When summer arrived, Mrs. Jones decided Bar Harbor, Maine, would be a safer haven for Edith than Newport, so she took Edith and her brother Harry north. The new home Freddy and Minnie had built there provided a perfect excuse to avoid Newport.

That Bar Harbor summer of 1883 would remain fondly etched in Edith's memory. It was at Bar Harbor, a few months after her social humiliation, that Edith ran into two young gentlemen who would play major roles in her life. The first was Walter Berry, a new acquaintance who would become, in Edith's own words, "the Love of all my life."

The second gentleman she would marry.

FOUR

Sunshine in the House

She had been bored all the afternoon by Percy Gryce . . . but she . . .
must submit to more boredom . . . all on the bare chance that he might
ultimately decide to do her the honour of boring her for life.

The House of Mirth, *1905*

$\mathcal{E}$dith was attracted to twenty-four-year-old Walter Van Rensselaer Berry from the moment he showed up at Bar Harbor. It wasn't so much that he was strikingly handsome in his white linen suit and summer boater. Edith had been around handsome men before. It was the personality that lived behind the piercing blue eyes and brown mustache that drew her—his coolness, his sharp sense of humor, and the fact that, although he came from a well-to-do family, he had ambitions, plans to go into international law. At six foot three, he was ten inches taller than she was. "To talk with him was to soar up into the azure on the outspread wings of his intelligence, and look down, dizzily yet clearly, on all the wonders and glories of the world," she would write about a

Walter Berry. He was distantly
related to Lucretia.

character years later. It was just how she felt about Walter Berry.

Many men didn't share Edith's high opinion of him. They found Walter Berry coldly rational, a "shell . . . with nothing inside it." One man noticed a "chill from within" him that always seemed to be "lowering the temperature" of everyone around. Women, on the other hand, found him irresistible. But even though he noticed every attractive female, his attention was on Edith from the moment he arrived. After arranging to meet in the lobby, she and Walter would stroll along the veranda that ran along the outside of the posh hotel. They might go bicycling, or hiking on the mountain trails, or boating. When they were together, they talked endlessly. Two days before he was scheduled to leave for Washington, D.C., Walter and Edith spent the whole afternoon canoeing on the lake. They saw "a great deal of each other for a few weeks," Edith remembered, and it gave her "a fleeting hint of what the communion of kindred intelligences might be."

When the time came for Walter to leave, he could have changed his plans. He could have told Edith that he didn't want to be without her. He could have proposed. But he didn't. Precisely on schedule, Walter Berry simply walked out of her life.

Whatever pain or confusion Edith felt, she endured it silently. During this time before her first published story, Edith was mentally gathering the material she would use in her writing, and years later, her characters would explore the possible reasons for an unexplained departure like Walter's. A professor in one story would speak of two kinds of women: "the fond and foolish, whom one married, and the earnest and intellectual, whom one did not." Was Edith that second kind of woman? Was her mother right to fear that Edith's intelligence would frighten off eligible bachelors?

In another story, a male character would think: "To have been loved by the most brilliant woman of her day, and to have been incapable of loving her, seemed to him . . . evidence of his limitations." Was the fault Walter's? Could it be that he was simply too cool and reasoned and in control to let himself fall in love?

All Edith knew for sure, that Bar Harbor summer, was that Walter Berry, like Harry Stevens, was not a marriage prospect. And Edith was twenty-one years old. Almost an old maid.

After Walter left for Washington, D.C., and his law career, another bachelor arrived at Bar Harbor. His name was Edward ("Teddy") Wharton. He was thirty-three, twelve years older than Edith, and a friend of her brother Harry's. Edith knew him well; he'd visited her family at Pencraig every year since she was eleven. He and Edith had an easy, teasing brother-sister relationship.

Where Walter was thin and a bit fragile, aloof, ambitious, and intelligent, Teddy was pure health and energy, gentle, warm, lighthearted, and thoroughly likable. He had no ambitions whatsoever. He'd graduated from Harvard, where he was known for being good-looking and for skipping classes. Teddy left hard work, success, and the serious side of life to his older brother, Billy, who eventually worked his way up to the position of Assistant Secretary of State under President Benjamin Harrison. That was all very well for Billy; Teddy preferred to focus on socializing, good food, good wine, hunting, and fishing.

Lucretia thought Teddy was "sunshine in the house." She also thought Edith needed to be married *soon*. Teddy was obviously not treating Edith like a little sister anymore, and Lucretia seized the moment. When the Joneses left Bar Harbor for Newport, Teddy went along with them. Lucretia broke her widow's habit of never entertaining and threw a dinner party for him that was elaborate enough to be mentioned in

Town Topics. That would show Mrs. Paran Stevens and the rest of New-port. The broken engagement to Harry Stevens had left the door open to someone more old-money and established.

Teddy was not, however, as cooperative a prospect as Lucretia had hoped. He was interested in Edith. In fact, he adored her. But after his visit to Newport, he quietly returned to Boston, where he lived with his mother and older sister, Nannie. Teddy's father had been institution-alized with some mysterious mental disorder, and these two women doted on Teddy. Perhaps they took too good care of him, pampering him and giving him an allowance to live on. Maybe he was so comfortable, he didn't think he needed a wife.

While Lucretia was waiting for Teddy to make his intentions known, Mrs. Stevens and the new-money people were busy battering away against Ward McAllister, Caroline Astor, and good Old New York soci-ety. Old-money people had claimed all the box seats worth having at the Academy of Music on East Fourteenth Street, so the new-money peo-ple built the Metropolitan Opera House on Thirty-ninth and Broadway. The newspapers had a field day when the new opera house opened in October 1883. One columnist said all the new-money people "were on hand . . . and . . . perfumed the air with the odor of crisp greenbacks." That evening, the Old Guard boycotted the new opera house and staunchly attended the performance at the Academy of Music. Mrs. Stevens had purchased seats in both places and spent the night shuttling between the two.

In January 1884, Teddy came to New York and escorted Edith to the Patriarchs' Ball. Mrs. Stevens was also at the ball. Harry wasn't—another victory for Lucretia. But after the ball, Teddy went back to Boston again. It took him another whole year, but finally, in January 1885, he proposed to Edith. By the time he popped the question, Lucretia had decided a long engagement was completely unnecessary and might even be dangerous. Edith was now twenty-three, and this

Edith and Teddy (right) in an engagement photo, taken on the lawn at Pencraig around 1884. The widowed Lucretia is dressed in black. Also shown are a cousin of Edith's (standing), a family friend, and two of the ever-present dogs.

could be her last opportunity to land a husband. Four months would be a long enough engagement. The wedding was set for April.

Teddy had no trouble choosing a best man and four ushers. He had plenty of friends. For Edith, finding bridesmaids was a definite problem. She loved her sister-in-law and her niece, but Minnie was in her thirties and too old, and Beatrix was only twelve and too young. Emelyn Washburn's eyes had gotten so bad she was nearly blind, not to mention the fact that she was close to thirty and still unmarried herself. Really, Lucretia decided, there was no need at all for bridesmaids. *Town Topics* disagreed. *Town Topics* "expected there would have been" bridesmaids at a society wedding. At this point Lucretia didn't care a fig what *Town Topics* expected.

Teddy's father didn't attend the wedding. The elder Mr. Wharton was too mentally unstable to leave the institution where he lived. Teddy's mother and sister assured Edith his affliction was not congenital. The doctors had told them so.

On April 29, 1885, Lucretia finally fulfilled her duty to her daughter. She got her married off. Just before noon, Edith stepped out of her mother's front door on West Twenty-fifth Street, wearing a white satin dress with a long court train, and crossed the street to Trinity Chapel. Her veil was fastened by a tiara glittering with the same diamonds Lucretia had worn when she married George Frederic. Lucretia had done right by Edith. She had sheltered her, protected her, kept her from all the low and unpleasant parts of life.

Lucretia had gotten her daughter to the altar, but she had not prepared her for the life that would follow. A few days before her marriage, Edith was "seized with such a dread of the whole dark mystery" that she begged her mother to tell her "what being married was like." Lucretia thought the question ridiculous and told Edith so. But Edith was desperate, so she persisted. "I'm afraid, Mamma—I want to know what will happen to me!" There was a silence. A long, dreadful silence. Lucretia's expression turned icy cold. "You've seen enough pictures & statues in your life," she said finally. "Haven't you noticed that men are—made differently from women?" Yes, Edith *had* noticed. Edith noticed everything. "Well, then—?" Lucretia demanded. Edith had no idea where her mother was going with this business about pictures and statues, so she politely waited for more explanation. "For heaven's sake don't ask me any more silly questions," Lucretia exploded. "You can't be as stupid as you pretend!" Edith was stunned. She was being ridiculed for not knowing the very thing she had always been forbidden to ask.

Years later, Edith would write of a new bride's "startled puzzled surrender to . . . the young man to whom one had at most yielded a rosy cheek in return for an engagement ring"; she would write of "the large double-bed" and the "terror" the new bride felt at seeing her new husband shaving. She would write of "resigned smiles . . . a week or a month of flushed distress, confusion, embarrassed pleasure." For Edith the "flushed distress" never turned into "embarrassed pleasure." The sexual side of her marriage to Teddy was a failure.

If they weren't a passionate couple, however, Edith and Teddy were at least good companions. Teddy's kindness softened the rough edges of Edith's personality, and he was clearly in love with her no matter what was lacking in the bedroom. The newlyweds had very little money according to the standards of what Mark Twain labeled the Gilded Age. Teddy received an allowance from his mother of about $2,000 a year (the equivalent of $46,000 today). Edith, who received about $10,000 a year ($230,000 today) from her father's inheritance, provided the majority of their income. She was also thoroughly in charge from day one.

The couple certainly couldn't afford to buy a house. They moved into Pencraig Cottage on Lucretia's Newport estate, where Freddy and Minnie had sometimes summered before building their cottage in Bar Harbor, Maine. Teddy and Edith would live there for the next eight years. It was at Pencraig Cottage that Edith created her first home and lovingly laid out her first garden. The year before her marriage, Edith had hired a goodhearted Alsatian woman named Catherine Gross as a maid. Communicating in French, Edith and "Gross" hired a staff of cooks and housemaids. Gross had a warmth Edith had never found in her mother, and she would remain with Edith for almost fifty years.

Treated almost like family were the small dogs—Pekingeses, Skye terriers, Pomeranians, poodles, and papillons—that Edith couldn't be without. They sat in her lap, rode with her in her carriage, and had their pictures taken with her. She spoiled them, had coats made for them by

• • •

*Pencraig Cottage was smaller than Pencraig, with only eight or ten rooms on
the first two floors and five or six servants' rooms on the third floor.*

a special dog knitter, and grieved when they died. The people closest to
her sometimes found her distant; but she communicated easily, almost
mystically, with her dogs.

Teddy was almost as fond of his wife's dogs as Edith herself was. Two
or three of them followed him when he visited Lucretia, trekking across
the property to his mother-in-law's house almost daily. Teddy loved
Newport and Newport loved Teddy. A story circulated that he once
hitched a ride in a butcher's cart right up the main street in order to
avoid being late for a luncheon date. A new-money fellow took him to
task for it: "I wouldn't do that if I were you," the man advised. Teddy responded, "No, if I were you I wouldn't do that either." He never flaunted
his wealth and privilege. He never gave his social position a thought. It
was simply a part of him.

Now that she was a year-round resident, Edith did not like Newport at all. During the couple's first summer there, Harry Stevens died in the local hospital. Most said it was tuberculosis that killed him. But one of the Rutherfords insisted Harry Stevens had died of a broken heart.

Also dead and gone were the slow, relaxed summers Edith remembered from her childhood. The new-money people had discovered the place, and as one of Edith's relatives observed, "the chief industry" had become the "business of granting, or withholding, social recognition." Along with the new-money set came the "confused din of dancing music, scandal, flirtation, serenades . . . singing, dancing, dawdling incessantly" and the "crushing into a month . . . that which crowds six months in town."

For Edith, the in season at Newport was empty and exhausting, and the off season was no better. When summer ended, the place became deserted, drafty, and soggy. For Edith, the off season meant prolonged struggles with asthma, bronchitis, and "an occult and unget-at-able nausea."

There were, however, two bright spots. One was a "new" friendship with a venerable old acquaintance of her parents', a widower named Egerton Winthrop. He was a high-society man through and through, but he was an *intelligent* society man. His quick mind sparked Edith's in the same way Walter Berry's had. Like Walter Berry, Egerton Winthrop believed in reason over imagination or emotion. "My new friend directed and systematized my reading, and filled some of the worst gaps in my education," Edith wrote of him. Egerton Winthrop took his mentoring task seriously. He told Edith what to read, introducing her to French literature, history, and literary criticism. He opened the door to the world of science. Charles Darwin's *On the Origin of Species*, which had scandalized the world when it was published three years before Edith's birth, was now widely accepted as fact and therefore a must-read. Edith hung on to her Bible and her Book of Common Prayer, but her new gods were Egerton Winthrop's: science and reason.

Egerton taught her how to approach a challenging book. She should read and reread slowly, make marginal notes when she came across something important, and mark things she didn't understand. He instructed her to think over each evening what she had read that day and jot down her ideas about it. She was a willing and eager pupil.

The second bright spot about Newport was getting away from it, which Teddy and Edith did for several months each spring. Italy was their usual destination, and Egerton Winthrop often went along with them. In Italy, they got about in a "heavy carriage drawn by tired horses." The horses were tired because they pulled Edith, her maid Gross, Egerton Winthrop, a small dog or two, and trunks full of clothes and books. While Edith, Egerton, and the maid inched along and took in the sights, Teddy, in another carriage, hurried on ahead to make arrangements for meals and an inn where they could spend the night. Teddy's was a difficult job, because Edith had high standards and complained loudly if the rooms didn't measure up.

It was Egerton Winthrop's job (also not an easy one) to bring Edith back down to reality. "My dear," he once told her, "no doubt your standards of cleanliness are higher than this hotel-keeper's; but I daresay the Princess of Wales . . . would not consider your toilet appointments good enough for her; and the angels may think even Her Royal Highness insufficiently clean." Egerton's playful scoldings usually worked. Whatever dirt and dust had offended Edith were pushed into the back of her mind, and her sense of adventure returned—until the travelers reached the next unsatisfactory inn on their route.

Wandering around Europe was something high-society people were expected to do, so the fact that Edith Wharton traveled was not unusual. But the particular spirit in which she traveled was. Edith's urge to see new places sprang directly out of her reading. While her wealthy friends

• • •

Edith, photographed in Newport several years after her marriage.
Reflecting her poor health in Newport, she looks thin and unhappy
in her fashionable leg-of-mutton sleeves.

yawned and nodded dutifully over the required tourist sights, Edith
wanted to find the unvisited places where the art and architecture and
history she knew from books lived. "With the open road before her,
dipping to some 'sparkling foreign country,'" a friend said of Edith the
traveler, "her heart leapt up—she was in her element; there was no such
blithe or purposeful traveler as Edith."

Unfortunately, after the annual European tour, it was back to soggy
old Newport, with occasional visits to Lucretia's place in New York. Back
to the shallow life of a society woman. By the time Edith married, that

VOL. 19 NO. 473   NOVEMBER 8 1890.   PRICE 10 CENTS.

Judge

SNOBBISH SOCIETY'S SCHOOLMASTER.
WARD McALLISTER.—"Uncle Sam, you must—aw—imitate this, or you will nevah be a gentleman!"

· · ·

This magazine cover was published several months before Ward McAllister's list came out. McAllister is shown with donkey ears, pointing to "an English snob" and telling a laughing Uncle Sam, "You must—aw—imitate this, or you will nevah be a gentleman!"

society life had changed dramatically from what it had been in her parents' day. The new-money Metropolitan Opera House had won out against the Academy of Music, which closed its doors in 1886. The Old Guard's insistence that money carried with it a certain responsibility and code of behavior had been completely swallowed up by the conspicuous consumption of the nouveau riche.

Caroline Astor and Ward McAllister refused to admit defeat. McAllister remarked that there were only about four hundred people who truly counted in New York society; only four hundred with sufficient birth, background, and breeding. The newspapers picked up on his comment, and everyone wanted to know who the four hundred were. They wanted names. Who was in and who was out? It took McAllister six years to come up with a list. While he was at it, at least one person of birth, background, and breeding was misbehaving badly—Edith's brother Freddy, who was caught by his wife, Minnie, in bed with another woman. The incident was carefully hushed up but not resolved.

Endless social events, Ward McAllister's list, adulterous affairs . . . most Newport/New Yorkers, those who were in and those who were out, loved keeping up with it all. For Edith, society balls and gossip were not enough to make life satisfying. She was losing weight, growing pale, and shriveling up mentally. In 1888, three years after her marriage to Teddy, she happened to remark to a friend named James Van Alen, "I would give everything I own to make a cruise in the Mediterranean!" Van Alen promptly offered to charter a yacht so that he and the Whartons could do just that. But how could Edith and Teddy take their friend up on his offer? The four-month cruise he was proposing would cost their entire year's income. What would they live on when they returned?

"Do you really want to go?" Teddy asked Edith.

She nodded.

"All right. Come along, then," he responded.

So off went the three—Edith, Teddy, and James Van Alen—stopping their ears to family members' prophecies of financial ruin. It was a dream of a trip, that cruise aboard the *Vanadis*—"the greatest step forward in my making," according to Edith. She got every bit of it down in her journal. While she lived each moment of those four months to the fullest, part of her stepped back and became a cool observer. She was as demanding a traveler as always. She was more than willing, however, to ride donkeys up steep slopes and enter exotic island villages where she herself was so exotic that crowds began "grasping the folds of my dress in their excited curiosity." She wrote of days when it was raining so hard "it was useless to go ashore, and so we stayed on the yacht, reading, writing and studying the Admiralty charts." And she basked in the sunshine of other days when "we sat on the bridge with white umbrellas over our heads."

The highlight of the trip was Mount Athos, a cluster of sacred monasteries in Greece. "The early established rule that no female, human or animal, is to set foot on the promontory, is maintained as strictly as ever," Edith wrote, "and as hens fall under this ban, the eggs for the monastic tables have to be brought all the way from Lemnos." Edith pushed the boundaries of this all-male world as far as she could. She had to remain on the yacht when Teddy and James visited the monasteries, but she ordered the captain to sail in as close as possible.

At first, the monks "sat in the sunshine watching me with evident curiosity." But "we went in so close to the shore that they clambered hurriedly down the hill to prevent my landing, and with their shocks of black hair and long woolen robes flying behind them they were a wild enough looking set to frighten any intruder away."

When she and Teddy picked up the mail in Athens near the end of their cruise, they learned that one of the dogs they'd left in New York had died. Edith was so devastated, she hardly noticed a second piece of news: Joshua Jones, a distant relative, had also died. He'd lived like a miser in an unheated room of a New York hotel, quietly accumulating a fortune, and he had left a huge sum of money to Edith and her brothers. The dark predictions that the cruise would be their financial undoing hadn't come true. Edith resolved never again to hesitate when she had the opportunity to do something "difficult and wonderful."

With the interest from her new inheritance, Edith's income far surpassed Teddy's. She paid James Van Alen in full for the trip. She hired a proper English butler named Alfred White for Teddy. And she scouted around for a home of her own. Lucretia had graciously let her use Pencraig Cottage, but Edith was ready for some independence. She rented a small house on Madison Avenue in New York City while she and Teddy looked for a place to buy.

Then she took an even bigger step: She ignored Egerton Winthrop's advice to begin the large-scale entertaining expected of a society matron and instead focused on her writing. Each morning she propped herself up in bed with a lapboard on her knees. She balanced an inkstand on the lapboard, spread books all over the bed, gathered her dogs around her for support, and took up her pen.

Edith decided to try her hand at poetry first and sent her work off to several magazines. Two weeks later, her efforts were rewarded. One poem was accepted by the *Atlantic Monthly* and two others by a newer but well-respected publication called *Scribner's Magazine*, an arm of the publishing firm of Charles Scribner's Sons. "I shall never forget my sensations when I opened the first of the three letters, and learned that I was to appear in print. I can still see the narrow hall, the letter-box out of which I fished the letters, and the flight of stairs up and down which I ran, senselessly and incessantly, in the attempt to give my excitement some muscular outlet!" The poems that had been published when she was a young girl had appeared unsigned or under a pseudonym. That would not be the case this time. Edith Wharton had written these poems, and Edith Wharton's name would appear with them *in print*.

The first of the accepted poems was published in *Scribner's Magazine* in October 1889. It was called "The Last Giustiniani," a twelve-stanza adaptation of an old tale about a Venetian monk released from his vows to marry so that his family line wouldn't end.

Better, even, than the acceptances themselves were the words of a Mr. Edward L. Burlingame, the editor at *Scribner's Magazine*. "He not only accepted my verses, but (oh, rapture!) wanted to know what else I had written." Edith sent him a short story, called "Mrs. Manstey's View," about a poor woman who takes bold action to prevent a building project that will destroy her one joy: the view out her window. Though Mr. Burlingame admitted, "We cannot often use a sketch as slight as that which you have kindly sent us," he published it anyway. Edith's very first work of fiction appeared in *Scribner's Magazine* in July 1891. She was twenty-nine years old.

Several months after Edith's story appeared, society had its eyes on another publication: Six years had elapsed since Ward McAllister's remark that there were four hundred people who "counted" in New York society; now the list was finally being printed in the *New York Times*. Not surprisingly, since she had helped McAllister create it, Caroline Astor was on the list. Though birth, background, and breeding were supposed to be the determining factors, Mrs. Astor's opinion trumped the "three b's," and there were some surprises. The new-money Vanderbilts, who'd made a fortune investing in railroads, were on the list. "We have no right," Mrs. Astor explained, "to exclude those whom the growth of this great country has brought forward, provided they are not vulgar in speech and appearance. The time has come for the Vanderbilts." But Old Guard names predominated. Egerton Winthrop, Edith's mentor and traveling companion, was on the list. Freddy, Minnie, and twenty-year-old Beatrix were all on the list, even though Minnie had finally had enough of Freddy's affairs and he was living in Paris with his mistress. Edith was not on the list and seemed to take no note of it. Perhaps she sensed that the Gilded Age had reached its height and would soon begin to crumble. She had her own reasons for appreciating McAllister's list, however: It was a gold mine of story characters.

Four months after her debut as a writer of fiction, Edith purchased a house on Park Avenue in New York City. She was ready to put some

• • •

Land's End. Working with Ogden Codman, Edith designed the formal garden and the veranda enclosed by glass panels imported from Italy.

space between her home and her mother's, and the new house was about as far away from Lucretia as she could get without raising eyebrows. It was too small to accommodate Teddy and Edith and their servants, however, so they didn't actually move in until she was able to purchase the house next door to it as well. The two properties at 884 Park Avenue and Seventy-eighth Street became the Whartons' winter residence for the next ten years.

In 1893 she also bought a house in Newport, at the opposite end of town from Lucretia and Pencraig. Edith and Teddy called their new summer home Land's End. It was "an ugly wooden house with half an acre of rock," but Edith had high hopes for it. She planned to completely remodel it and plant her second garden.

Teddy knew a Boston architect, Ogden Codman, who agreed to renovate and decorate the place. It was remarkable that Codman was prepared to do both. Architects were respected in the 1890s, but interior decorators were on the same low social level as dressmakers. Edith had no use for conventional decorators who disregarded the structure of a room and, in Edith's words, filled every corner with "wobbly velvet-covered tables . . . and festoons of lace." Edith loathed the way her mother's generation hid a house's architecture under a bunch of things. She thought houses, like people, should be honest about what they were. Ogden Codman agreed with her, and they worked terrifically together. They turned Edith's Newport home into a fresh, comfortable place different from both the white wood cottages of the Old Guard and the showy mansions of the swells.

After the two completed their work, one of the first visitors to Land's End was a writer. A real writer.

FIVE

New Writer Who Counts

*Sometimes I feel as if the sea, and the cliffs, and the skyline
out there, were all a part of the stupid show—the expensive stage setting
of a rottenly cheap play—to be folded up and packed away with the rest
of the rubbish when the performance is over.*

"The Introducers," short story, 1905

In 1893, just after Edith and Teddy were comfortably settled at Land's End for the summer season, a Frenchman named Paul Bourget visited Newport with his wife, Minnie. He had been commissioned by the *New York Herald* to write about his impressions of America. His novels, poetry, and essays were well known in France. Newport society was eager to meet him; he was asked to lunches and dinners and balls and sporting events and yachting excursions.

His opinion of America could be summed up in two words: too much! "The American spirit seems not to understand moderation," he observed. There was, to begin with, too much coming and going and doing. Days were packed so full of leisure activities that everyone was left exhausted. And as for the houses of these too-energetic Americans, "On the floors of halls which are too high there are too many precious Persian and Oriental rugs. There are too many tapestries, too many paintings . . . too much rare furniture . . . too many flowers, too many plants, too much crystal, too much silver." This visiting Frenchman was amused by Ward McAllister's attempt to "establish an artificial Olympus, that of the 'four hundred,' which are drawn from the families of oldest traditions and most wealth." What in the world did these Americans know about old traditions? Or about the generations it took to make real nobility? Unlike French aristocracy, the ancestors of Ward McAllister's illustrious four hundred were pioneers, shopkeepers, and poor immigrants. These elite Americans were not "born to social station; they have achieved it," Bourget concluded.

When his investigation of Newport took him to lunch at Land's End, his neat conclusions were upset. Land's End was a unique island of calm and good taste in the midst of all Newport's hectic, shallow activity. Land's End seemed almost European. It was a place that had a sense of tradition; it was filled with impressive books that looked very much as if they'd been read and not just ordered by the yard for decoration. It didn't take Paul Bourget long to determine who had read those books. It was not the master of the house but his wife, Edith Wharton.

Conversation between the Whartons and the Bourgets over lunch that summer day was comical. Minnie Bourget spoke good English, but Paul kept making hilarious mistakes. Edith's old-fashioned French made Paul laugh. But her French was better than the French Teddy spoke, which was none. The language mistakes on all sides made everyone comfortable, and the talk flowed to books and ideas and then to writing. Paul Bourget was the first real writer Edith had ever met, and she wanted him to know she could hold her own in an intelligent conversation. Egerton Winthrop, after all, had made sure she'd read the right things and read them thoroughly.

Perhaps Egerton had done his job too well. In one of the pieces Paul Bourget later wrote about America, he described an American character, the "intellectual tomboy, the girl who is up to the times, who has read everything, understood everything, not superficially, but really, with an energy of culture that could put to shame the whole Parisian fraternity of letters." Such a woman made him long for "one ignorance, one error, just a single one." Could he have had Edith in mind when he wrote these words? Edith would have shuddered to think that this was the impression she was making. But whatever Paul Bourget wrote later, the two couples thoroughly enjoyed each other's company and made plans to meet the next time the Whartons were in Europe.

• • •

Paul and Minnie Bourget in September 1893. Detail of photo courtesy of the Isabella Stewart Gardner Museum, Boston.

Paul Bourget's visit to Land's End inspired Edith. Three stories were on Mr. Burlingame's desk at Scribner's by the end of October, and her editor responded with a proposal: He would publish the stories she'd sent in *Scribner's Magazine* and, when she'd written a few more, publish them all in a book. Edith replied, "I need hardly say how much I am flattered by Messrs. Scribner's [*sic*] proposition to publish my stories in a volume."

What she didn't tell Mr. Burlingame was that his proposal threw her into a panic. She was having second thoughts about one of the three stories she'd sent to *Scribner's Magazine*. It was called "The Fulness of Life," and it was about a woman who chooses to stay married to a dull man who doesn't understand her. The husband in the story has boots that "creaked, and he always slammed the door when he went out, and he never read anything but railway novels and the sporting advertisements in the papers." Would people think she was describing Teddy? "I have sometimes thought," the woman in the same story observes, "that a woman's nature is like a great house full of rooms: there is the hall, through which everyone passes in going in and out; the drawing-room, where one receives formal visits; the sitting-room, where the members of the family come and go." But beyond all the rooms filled with people, there was another room, "the innermost room, the holy of holies." In that room, the woman thinks, "the soul sits alone and waits for a foot-step that never comes." When it appeared in the magazine, that story left Edith feeling exposed. She absolutely would not allow it to be reprinted. But if she didn't use it, could she come up with enough additional stories to fill a whole book? And was she a writer, after all? Or was she just a society lady who happened to crank out a few stories?

For the moment, she chose to be a society lady. She and Teddy sailed for Europe in December 1893 and called on the Bourgets in Paris. They traveled through Tuscany, and Edith sent Mr. Burlingame an article about some sculptures she'd stumbled upon in a monastery. *Scribner's Magazine* published the article and Edith felt safe. Nonfiction was less revealing than fiction.

"I seem to have fallen into a period of groping. . . . I have lost confidence in myself at present," she wrote Mr. Burlingame from Florence the following March. And then, three months later, "If Messrs. Scribners still want to publish a volume of my stories . . . I should rather have another six months in which to prepare it." Then she stopped writing to Mr. Burlingame altogether.

By the time Edith returned to New York, Minnie and Beatrix Jones were the only close family members still living in the city. Harry and

Ogden Codman designed, remodeled, or decorated more than a hundred houses over the course of his career. His contacts with the very wealthy gave him lots to gossip about in his letters to his mother.

Freddy had both moved to Paris. Lucretia had decided she wanted to live near her sons and was moving to Paris also. So it wasn't her family's expectations that kept Edith from writing the stories for which Mr. Burlingame was waiting. It was something inside her.

She threw herself into redecorating Land's End, with the help—again—of Ogden Codman. In December 1895 she finally sent Mr. Burlingame a letter full of excuses and apologies. "Since I last wrote you over a year ago, I have been very ill," it began. This was a bit dramatic. Her bouts with flu had not curtailed her traveling in the least. With the letter, she sent what she called a poor "waif" of a story, which Mr. Burlingame promptly rejected. Once again she took refuge in nonfiction. She seized on the love of interior design she shared with Ogden Codman. "Finding that we had the same views we drifted, I hardly know how, toward the notion of putting them into a book." So instead of working on short stories, she began a book on home decorating.

Edith took an eight-month trip to Europe in 1896 to do research for the book. With Teddy following along dutifully, she combed Italy looking for grand villas and castles. She was in France twice during these months, but her relationship with her mother and Freddy had turned icy. Freddy and Minnie were now officially divorced. Edith took Minnie's side and refused to have anything to do with her brother's mistress. Nothing in society's rule book told Lucretia how to behave toward a divorced son; divorce wasn't supposed to happen in proper families, and the trauma of the whole thing was affecting her health.

• • •

The busy, cluttered interior of Lucretia's New York home on West Twenty-fifth Street (top) is a stark contrast to the simple, light style of Edith's home on Park Avenue, decorated according to the principles she and Ogden Codman championed in their book.

But she chose to stand by Freddy, and that put her at odds with Edith. The venerable Jones family had broken into warring pieces.

Throughout her travels, Edith peppered Codman with letters describing the information she was gathering for their book and asking what he thought about her Park Avenue house, which he was also helping to renovate. What could be done with the pantry and the plumbing?

Back in Newport in the fall of 1896, she sat down to begin *The Decoration of Houses*, only to find that "I literally could not write out in simple and precise English the ideas which seemed so clear in my mind." Codman was no help. His writing was rambling and gossipy, and he didn't seem to know that a sentence should *end* at some point. He said he would come to Newport, then didn't show up. He didn't answer her letters. She was at the end of her patience with him. "I regret very much that I undertook the book," she wrote to him. "I certainly should not have done so if I had not understood that you were willing to do half. . . . I hate to put my name to anything so badly turned out." But then, miraculously, help arrived in the form of a long-lost friend.

It had been fourteen years since Walter Berry had spent those wonderful weeks with Edith at Bar Harbor and left with no comment on their relationship. During those fourteen years, he'd established a law practice in Washington, D.C., and Edith had seen him only in passing. But in late July 1897, when he was thirty-seven and she was thirty-five, he came to Land's End for a month-long visit. He hadn't proposed to Edith at Bar Harbor, but he hadn't proposed to anyone else in the years since. He was still a bachelor, he still had an eye for beautiful women, he still looked dashing.

And he was still wonderfully quick and intelligent. Would Walter be able to help her with *The Decoration of Houses*? "I remember shyly asking him to look at my lumpy pages," Edith wrote in her autobiography. "I remember his first shout of laughter (for he never flattered or pretended), and then his saying good-naturedly: 'Come, let's see what can be done,' and settling down beside me to try to model the lump into a book. In a few weeks the modelling was done, and in those weeks, as I afterward discovered, I had been taught whatever I know about the writing of clear concise English." By late August, Walter declared the book fit for publication. Scribner's agreed to publish it, and Edith had a hand in every stage of the process. She found many of the photos, helped with the design and printing, prepared the bibliography, and arranged to have the book reviewed in the major magazines. Walter Berry had polished her writing; her negotiations with a Mr. William Brownell, a literary consultant at Scribner's, turned her into a skilled book designer and businesswoman.

The Decoration of Houses—her very first book—came out in early December 1897, just in time for Christmas. The one thousand copies that were printed sold out in a matter of months. A review in the *Bookman* called it a work of "large insight." The reviewer was none other than Walter Berry.

The Decoration of Houses was Edith's first public jab at the suffocating world in which she'd grown up. For now, it was the setting—the "small townhouses" with their "exquisite discomfort"—that she focused on. It would be eight years before she

• • •

Edith in 1897, when Walter Berry reentered her life.

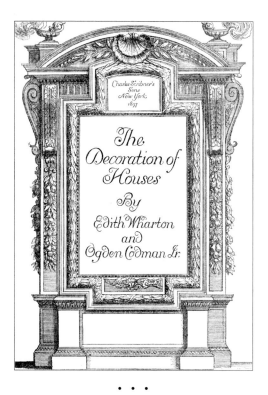

The title page to Edith's first book, The Decoration of Houses. *It is considered a classic work on interior design.*

would take aim at the people of that world. And when she did, she would do it in a novel.

The glowing success of *The Decoration of Houses* took the chill off her relationship with Ogden Codman, at least for a time. It didn't succeed in warming up Newport, however. She and Teddy had to stay on into the winter months because renovations were being done on their New York home. She was miserably ill and couldn't seem to shake whatever it was that had hold of her. "I hate to think so but I believe this place does not agree with her," Teddy wrote to Codman. By Christmas, Teddy finally managed to move his sick wife to New York City, where she began to recover.

Safely away from Newport, Edith wrote a wonderful little story called "The Pelican." The heroine, Mrs. Amyot, seems to be a version of Paul Bourget's "intellectual tomboy," but in this case "there was nothing she did not remember—wrongly." Her "facts were swathed in so many layers of rhetoric that their infirmities were imperceptible."

With its publication in *Scribner's Magazine* in November 1898, Edith, at the age of thirty-seven, seemed to hit her stride as a writer. She showed Walter almost everything she wrote, and he knew just when to encourage and when to offer advice. "He followed each of my literary steps with the same patient interest, and I doubt if a beginner in the art ever had a sterner yet more stimulating guide." Walter saw her talent, and he was not at all repelled by her writer's ambitions. Edith had plenty of social friends; Walter Berry was the first to be a friend to her writing.

With Walter's help, she selected the stories that would be included in the long-delayed short story collection for Scribner's. There were now so many to choose from that Edith didn't even have to consider the one about the husband with squeaky boots. She described that story as "one long shriek" and was glad to have it behind her.

Edith's book of short stories—*The Greater Inclination*—came out in March 1899. It was populated by ambitious characters, unhappy wives, and women who wanted romance but found themselves in intellectual friendships instead. Edith waited for the reviewers to pass judgment on it; perhaps they'd be kinder than she had been to herself as a fifteen-year-old. They were. When the reviews appeared, Anna Bahlmann, once Edith's governess and now her secretary, carefully pasted them in a scrapbook. Under the headline "New Writer Who Counts," one critic declared, "We have seen nothing this year that has impressed us so much as Mrs. Wharton's book." It seemed she really was capable of doing what she'd always dreamed of: writing fiction.

"At last I had groped my way through to my vocation, and thereafter I never questioned that story-telling was my job," she wrote in her autobiography. "I felt like some homeless waif who, after trying for years to take out naturalization papers, and being rejected by every country, has finally acquired a nationality. The Land of Letters was henceforth to be my country, and I gloried in my new citizenship."

She took up her pen quietly, almost secretly, in bed, in the early hours of each day. Every morning, whether at home or traveling, Edith became the classic picture of the solitary writer. Every morning she reached for her lapboard, gathered her dogs (currently the papillons Miza and Mimi and a Skye terrier named Jules) on the covers around her, and lost herself in her writing.

Although she guarded her morning working hours, she didn't permit them to intrude on her other activities. A friend observed, "Her

• • •

Teddy in 1898 with Jules, Miza, and Mimi.

work was not her life—it had to fit in with very much else, and she cut out nothing for its sake." That friend saw so much of the active side of Edith Wharton that he wondered how she managed to get anything written at all. "Her books, growing in the privacy of which there seemed to be so little, appeared in their succession with increasing freedom and assurance—the books of a writer who evidently loved every moment of her work and every nicety of her craft . . . who would ever think, reading her books, that they were written in the bare margin of such a populous and ornamental existence."

Each day, around noon, Edith would lay her lapboard aside and step out of her bedroom, dressed smartly, with her hair done, glad to meet the world and its inhabitants. She loved to have fun and she knew how to laugh. "I can see her," another friend remembered, "speechless with shoulders shaking and the tears running down her cheeks." To strangers and casual acquaintances, Edith could appear too prim and proper—severe, even. But those in her inner circle saw the joy and energy with which she lived her life.

Two months after the publication of her short story collection, she and Teddy were off to London. There, Edith wandered into a bookstore and asked for something interesting to read. The bookseller, having no idea who she was, handed her a book: *The Greater Inclination* by Edith Wharton. "This is what everybody in London is talking about just now," he told her. Edith was astounded. "Any one walking along the streets might go into any bookshop, and say: 'Please give me Edith Wharton's book,' and the clerk, without bursting into incredulous laughter, would produce it."

From London, Edith and Teddy crossed over to the Continent, joined forces with Paul and Minnie Bourget, and set out to explore an area called the Bergamasque Alps, near the city of Bergamo in northern Italy. Paul, the dapper Frenchman, rode in the carriage with the ladies while Teddy, the American outdoorsman, traveled ahead (on a bicycle this time) to make arrangements. The foursome covered nearly a hundred miles of rugged, mountainous terrain. As they traveled and talked, Paul Bourget encouraged Edith to seek out people "who were thinking and creating." He insisted that the society part of her life was nothing more than "wearisome frivolity."

Edith later remembered those weeks in Switzerland and northern Italy as the happiest of her life. She was healthy (because she was away from Newport), she was finally a real writer, she was in the company of a real writer, and she had Walter Berry back in Washington, D.C., ready to offer support. And even if Teddy's boots squeaked, he was the sunniest of traveling companions.

But the best journeys end and travelers must return home. In September 1899, Edith wrote to her editor from Land's End that her health had been fine "till our return to Newport; but the dampness here—we are having mid-summer fogs—is making me as unhappy as usual." Finally at the end of her rope, she and Teddy and the dogs and the servants packed up and moved to Teddy's mother's summer home in Lenox, Massachusetts, while the elder Mrs. Wharton and Teddy's unmarried sister, Nannie, were out of town. Walter Berry wrote that he was glad she'd gotten away from "all that sogginess." Newport was like a bad habit she was having trouble breaking. When Walter learned she was headed back there in November, he warned: *"Don't, don't go back."* But she did, and with the usual results. "I do wish you would take my advice just occasionally," he complained.

The Whartons' European trip in the spring of 1900 was a bittersweet experience. Edith and Teddy stayed with the Bourgets in Paris, and Edith, more dutifully than lovingly, visited her sick mother each day. Edith still loved her brother Harry but would barely speak to Freddy or the disreputable woman he'd now married. Her loyalties were to Minnie and Beatrix. Lucretia was on fine terms with Freddy, but she wouldn't speak to Harry because he'd legally adopted Beatrix to protect her inheritance in the wake of the divorce. And neither Minnie nor Beatrix Jones, both living in New York, was on good terms with Freddy. But this gathering in Paris was as together as the Jones family would ever be again. A few weeks after Edith's visit, Lucretia fell into a coma.

Returning to Land's End, which Walter called "never never well land," Edith was sick within twenty-four hours. She had finally had enough. It was time to exchange the ocean for the mountains. She and Teddy leased Land's End out for the season and rented a house in Lenox, the town where they'd stayed in Teddy's mother's summer home the year before. Teddy set out on a long yacht trip with a friend, and Edith let the wonderful Berkshire Mountains work their healing magic. She

• • •

*Teddy in the foreground, Edith farther back, and two dogs exploring the property on which the
Mount would be built. Edith named her new home after the estate of her great-grandfather.*

rode a new horse Teddy had given her. Walter visited and found Edith
looking wonderful. "The truth is," she wrote to Ogden Codman from
Lenox, "I am in love with the place—climate, scenery, life and all."

And in the mornings, as always, she wrote. She was supposed to be
at work on a second volume of short stories, but, as she confessed to
William Brownell, her literary consultant at Scribner's, she had laid the
short story project aside and begun a novel, *The Valley of Decision*. "The
thing has taken hold of me so that I can't get away from it," she wrote.
But three months later, still at Lenox, still writing, she sent him another
letter: "Don't think me a monster of inconsistency. . . . After doing over
40,000 words of The Valley without a break I suddenly found the tank
empty." She had gone back to work on the short story collection.

She was particularly proud of one story she planned to include, "The Line of Least Resistance." It had appeared in *Lippincott's Magazine*, and she thought it was the best story she'd ever written. She liked it so much, she sent a copy to a famous writer she was dying to get to know, Henry James.

Henry James was a New Yorker who now lived in England. He was at the peak of his literary career, and Edith particularly admired two of his novels, *Daisy Miller* and *The Portrait of a Lady*. Edith knew people who knew Henry James, people such as Paul Bourget and her sister-in-law, Minnie Jones. She had been at dinner parties with James, but the great man had never noticed her, even though she'd worn clothes that she thought might catch his attention. Maybe Henry James would be impressed with "The Line of Least Resistance," a story about a society man who refuses to confront his wife about the affair she's having.

In the meantime, there was business to attend to: She had to escape—finally—from soggy, frivolous Newport. In November 1900, Edith and Teddy traveled to Land's End to close it up. Though they didn't sell it for another three years, they would never live in it again. By spring of 1901 she'd purchased a 113-acre lot in Lenox, where she intended to build the perfect house from the ground up. It would be large and light filled and decorated according to the principles she and Ogden Codman had set out in their book. It would be surrounded by beautiful gardens. It would be called the Mount.

· SIX ·

A Republic of the Spirit

She sought in vain among her companions for an answering mind.

The Valley of Decision, *1902*

In the fall of 1900, a letter arrived from Henry James—*the* Henry James. The carefully chosen clothes Edith had worn to dinner parties hadn't attracted his notice, but her story had. He had not only read "The Line of Least Resistance," he'd taken the time to send her comments about it. Edith just couldn't quite understand them. Henry James had a way of circling around whatever he wanted to say: "I applaud, I mean I value, I egg you on in your study of the human life that surrounds you," he wrote. But then he added that the story was "a little *hard.*" What did he mean by that? Edith showed Henry's letter to Walter, who couldn't make any more out of it than she could. But the last sentence she did understand: "Do, some day, better still, come to see yours, dear Mrs.

• • •

The Mount, seen from the walled garden. Edith's niece, Beatrix, who helped her
design the original grounds, became one of America's first female landscape architects.

Wharton, most truly, Henry James." It was an open invitation to visit
him in England.

But the visit would have to wait. By February 1901, she was spending most of her time in Lenox supervising the building of the Mount.
Unfortunately, she didn't make a good first impression on all her future
neighbors. The very story that caught Henry James's attention mightily offended Mrs. William Sloane, the former Emily Vanderbilt and
reigning social queen of Lenox. Mrs. Sloane was not amused by "The
Line of Least Resistance." She was convinced that the character in the

story who has an affair was a thinly disguised version of her former sister-in-law. Edith tried to smooth things over. She told her editor the story could not be included in *Crucial Instances,* her second short story collection, and she scrambled to find a story to replace it. When *Crucial Instances* came out (without "The Line of Least Resistance"), a reader was upset by another story about an affair that Edith had included. "Dear Madam," the reader wrote. "Have you never known a respectable woman? If you have, in the name of decency write about her!"

Then there were problems at the Mount. Teddy didn't like the rough sketches Ogden Codman had drawn. Both Teddy and Edith thought Codman was overcharging them. Codman decided the Whartons would wear him "to a shadow with their nonsense" and "fussing" and was annoyed that they wouldn't spend as much as his other *very* rich clients. Teddy flew into a rage, which surprised everyone but Ogden Codman. Codman had known the Wharton family for a very long time and had watched Teddy's father slowly go insane. Codman decided Teddy was on the same path as his father. "Teddy Wharton seems to be losing his mind," he wrote to his mother. "He looks very old and broken and has lost most of his hair on the top of his head."

Edith thought Teddy's fit was nothing more than an isolated incident and entirely justified by Codman's behavior. In the end, the Whartons hired another architect. Walter thought they were "dead right in chucking" Codman. Codman retaliated by spewing out poisonous gossip. He wasn't entirely sure, he told his mother, but he strongly suspected Edith was a wife to Teddy "in name only." He also told his mother that Edith's "story about the Sloanes finished her with all the Sloane Vanderbilt hangers on who are now hacking at her like a lot of yellow dogs."

On top of offended neighbors and a gossipy ex-architect, the news came that Edith's mother had died in Paris. Lucretia hadn't exactly cut Edith out of her will, but the terms of her bequest to her daughter were not what Edith expected. Her brothers got lump sums of money, Harry much less than Freddy because he was on the outs with his mother. Edith's portion was a trust fund controlled by her brothers. Edith trusted Harry to take care of her estate, but she didn't trust Freddy, who had left Minnie and Beatrix struggling financially after the divorce. So Edith and Teddy traveled to Paris and with Harry's help forced Freddy to turn his trustee responsibilities over to Teddy. It was all very wearing. "I excessively hate to be forty," Edith wrote to a friend just after her birthday. "Not that I think it a bad thing to be—only I'm not ready yet!"

That year—1902—turned out to have good things in store for Edith. In February, *The Valley of Decision*, her first full-length novel, came out. The hero, Odo, becomes duke of one of the crumbling feudal principalities of eighteenth-century Italy. A champion of reason and new ideas, Odo tries to set his subjects free from the tyranny of the Catholic Church, only to learn that they prefer authority and structure to freedom. It might have been a picture of Edith's relationship to society. She tested the limits of society's rules and regulations, but she also appreciated the stability it provided.

Edith was afraid the two-dollar price tag (equivalent to fifty dollars today) on her new two-volume book would frighten buyers away. She thought such an expensive book by a new novelist was "an impertinence." The price didn't scare Henry James away. He managed to lay his hands on a copy and was impressed with it. He sent Edith a letter telling her so. But, he complained, *The Valley of Decision* was a historical novel set in a foreign country, and this, Henry James wrote, was not what Edith should be writing. He urged her "earnestly, tenderly, intelligently . . . in favour of the American subject. There it is round you. Don't pass it by—the immediate, the real, the only, the yours, the novelist's that it waits for. Take hold of it and keep hold, and let it pull you where it will. . . . *Do New York!*" Although Henry James didn't know it, Edith had already taken his advice. She was busy jotting things down about the New York of her childhood in a little notebook. Those jottings would grow, over the next three years, into the novel that would make her famous.

The Mount still wasn't finished by the fall of 1902, but Edith and Teddy moved in anyway. Of course Ogden Codman felt obliged to have a low opinion of the place. *"Really it is a pity* to have it turn out so forlorn," he told his mother. "The Whartons know just enough to be very *unhappy* but not enough to get anything done right, they have always supposed they knew all they knew and all I knew too. *Now they realize they don't.*"

• • •

A light-filled hallway near the rear entrance to the Mount.

Others didn't share his opinion. William and Emily Vanderbilt Sloane abandoned their disapproval and came to the housewarming. Guests that day and those who enjoyed Edith and Teddy's hospitality at the Mount in later years found the house impressive. It had thirty-five rooms, including eight rooms for servants on the top floor and three guest rooms on the second floor. Edith had her own suite, which could be closed off from the rest of the house so she could do her morning writing without interruption. One guest saw the Mount as a reflection of Edith Wharton the artist, "content with nothing less than the best in the gardening, the cooking, the furnishing and housekeeping of her place. Everything in it was harmonious."

Overseeing the Whartons' staff were their two servants, Alfred White, the English butler, and Catherine Gross, Edith's maid. White served "with respectful severity." Balancing White's seriousness was Gross, "with her wise old puckered face and crumpled smile." She was simply "everywhere" in her quest to make things right for Edith. These two—White and Gross—were the core of a household staff who would faithfully serve her for years.

Now that Edith had built a world according to her exacting standards, it was time to populate that world—also according to her standards. She could tolerate shallow society gatherings to a point, but what she really wanted was stimulating conversation. Some of the people who lived near the Mount were intelligent enough to provide it. Edith had made friends with a woman named Sally Norton who lived with her father, Charles Eliot Norton, a retired Harvard professor, forty miles away in Ashfield. But most of her neighbors weren't sure whether they liked Edith or not. Stories about her uppity comments flew around Lenox. Many suspected Edith might use them as characters in her next story.

So Edith imported her company, inviting carefully chosen guests for visits that might last a weekend or several weeks. Teddy and Edith were the perfect host and hostess. "What an amusing and delightful

• • •

Teddy on his horse at the Mount, holding his dog Jules.

house it was to stay in," said one guest. Another called the hospitality "abundant" and the talk "sparkling." If there was a complaint, it was that the place was a little *too* perfect . . . cold, perhaps. Sally Norton's younger sister, Lily, thought the Mount was lacking children and large romping dogs. She didn't feel the miniature breeds Edith favored counted as *real* dogs. But to most, everything about Edith's life looked flawless. She had the Mount for summers, a house in New York for winters, a dashing husband who doted on her, and a writing career that was beginning to take off.

Just beneath the surface of that perfect life, however, lurked concern about Teddy's new outbursts and moodiness. Soon after the housewarming party at the Mount, he had a kind of breakdown that turned him gloomy and dark. "I am bothered about him," Edith told Sally Norton. Ogden Codman, who always had Teddy's father's condition in the back of his mind, supposed Edith's plan was to put off committing Teddy to an asylum for as long as possible, "as he will probably never get any better."

But Edith assumed, and Teddy's mother and sister insisted, that his problems were physical, not mental. The doctors suggested that Edith and Teddy should go immediately to someplace sunny and warm. Since Edith had just been commissioned by *Century Magazine* to write the text for a book featuring watercolors of Italian villas, Italy looked like the perfect place for the Whartons to visit.

The Italian tour did nothing for Teddy's health. He continued to complain about various aches and pains, and his mood was dismal. In spite of her ailing husband, Edith focused on the writing of *Italian Villas and Their Gardens*, and she "never enjoyed any work more than the preparing of that book." It was certainly more physically demanding than the story writing she did in bed each morning. "The day of the motor was not yet," she remembered in her autobiography. "Most of the places I wished to visit were far from the principal railway lines, and could be reached only by a combination of slow trains and broken-down horse conveyances."

One tour was strikingly different. An old friend named George Meyer, who was the American ambassador in Rome, offered to take Edith and Teddy by "motor" to one of the villas on Edith's list. Teddy and the chauffeur were "put behind" in the back seat. The ambassador drove, and Edith took the high seat beside him. Edith remembered every detail of her very first ride in an automobile. "I climbed proudly to my perch, and off we tore across the Campagna, over humps and bumps, through ditches and across gutters, wind-swept, dust-enveloped, I clinging to my sailor-hat, and George Meyer (luckily) to the wheel. We did the run in an hour, and . . . tore back to Rome, in time for a big dinner." She swore then and there that as soon as she could afford it, she would purchase her own motor.

After the Italian trip, the Whartons returned to the Mount. Edith was not entirely happy to be there. Teddy was still sunk in his dark mood. Europe had stirred Edith's heart when she was a child and now had a firm hold on her. Europe was where she wanted to be. She wrote to Sally about how miserable she always was her first few weeks back in America, how she felt "more acutely than ever the contrast between the old & the new." She and Sally were like two "wretched" flowers transported to America from a European greenhouse. In her journal, she copied a quote from a French novel she was reading: "Her life was as cold as a garret whose windows face north, and boredom like a spider spun its web in the shadows, to all the corners of her heart." One positive note was a new novella, *Sanctuary*, that came out in 1903. But it was a depressing story about a morally sensitive woman who discovers a character flaw in the man she loves. It could well have drawn on the disillusionment Edith was feeling about her own marriage.

Two months after it was published, she and Teddy

. . .

When Henry James (left) and Howard Sturgis (right)
visited the Mount in 1904, Teddy (center)
was a gracious and congenial host.

were off to Europe again. England and the long-awaited face-to-face meeting with Henry James would be the first order of business. "The Master," as Henry James was sometimes called, left his home in Rye, in southeastern England, to join the Whartons at their London hotel for the afternoon. Describing the meeting to Minnie Jones, Henry wrote: "I mustn't omit to tell you . . . that Mrs. Wharton has come and gone—gone, alas. . . . I lunched with her, with very great pleasure, and had the opportunity of some talk. This gave me much desire for more—finding her, as I did, really conversible (rare characteristic . . .) and sympathetic in every way. I count greatly on her return." Edith found in Henry James the perfect mixture of humor and elegance, and she was relieved to discover that he talked far more clearly than he wrote.

After ten days in England, the Whartons crossed the channel to France, where Edith used her earnings from *The Valley of Decision* to purchase, as she told Sally in a letter, "a motor-car of moderate speed and capacious dimensions." Edith's new plaything made Henry James grumpy. He was a much more highly respected writer than Edith, but he never seemed to be able to make money from his writing the way Edith could. And here was Edith, the young upstart, buying a car with the proceeds from her first novel. "With the proceeds of *my* last novel," Henry groused, "I purchased a small go-cart. . . . It needs a coat of paint. With the proceeds of my next I shall have it painted."

Whatever Henry James thought, Edith and Teddy meant to enjoy their new toy.

• • •

The garden room of Henry James's home in Rye, England. The secretary to whom he dictated his novels here each morning thoroughly disliked Edith because her visits disrupted Henry's writing routine.

The depression that had descended on Teddy a year earlier suddenly lifted, and he drove the motor from Paris to the south of France to break it in while Edith followed by train. Then Edith and Teddy hopped into the car together and took off with gusto, Teddy (restored to his usual cheerfulness) wearing goggles and a canvas coat, Edith in a long cape with a chiffon scarf over her head. Edith fell on this new contraption as though, in the words of a friend, "it had been invented for her." She didn't understand it as a machine, but she fully understood its power to move her from place to place. "While others were still petting or humouring it," the friend observed, "she trailed the cloud of her dust along the open highways, she threaded the green lanes that were still startled by the strange new beast."

The new motor, of course, had to be shared and shown off, and who better to share with and show off to than their new friend Henry James? The Whartons and their motor ferried across the English Channel, and Henry traveled by train to meet them at the English coast and guide them to his house in Rye. "Guide" is perhaps not the right term. For all his skill with words, Henry James had no sense of direction. Even when Rye, set up on its hill, was plainly in sight, they circled round and round it and arrived at James's property, Lamb House, well after dark.

This was the first of many visits Edith would make to Lamb House. Henry "lived in terror of being thought rich, worldly or luxurious" and his house showed it. Outside was the "thin worn turf of the garden, with its ancient mulberry tree" and its "unkempt flower borders." Inside was a "white-panelled hall," full of "old prints" and "crowded book-cases." Some rickety steps led to the garden room where, every morning, Henry paced back and forth, dictating his novels to his secretary.

When Edith and Teddy left Europe that year, they had to leave their wondrous French automobile behind. Arriving at the Mount for the summer, they immediately bought a "little sputtering shrieking American motor." Actually, they purchased a whole series of motorcars, "for

• • •

In this 1904 photograph, Henry James and Edith are in the back seat of the Whartons' Pope Hartford automobile. Cook, the chauffeur, dressed in black, and Teddy are in the front.

in those days it was difficult to find one which did not rapidly develop some organic defect."

They also hired a chauffeur, Charles Cook, a man with mechanical skill, an unerring sense of direction, and an unflappable temperament. A friend of Edith's called Cook "grandly calm." Cook became another of the servants who were family. Edith trusted him completely. But it was terribly difficult for her to sit in the back seat while someone else han-

dled all the *doing* in the front seat. So while Cook drove, Edith partici-
pated by barraging him with questions: Were they going the right way?
And wasn't the motor sounding oddly? And where in the world was the
map? And was he entirely sure that last turn was right? Cook was always
good-humored and composed. Nothing shook him—not even Edith's
"help."

Somehow, in the middle of her travels and her entertaining at the
Mount, Edith continued to reach for her lapboard and pen each morning. Wherever she was, she found time to write. She kept notebooks full
of ideas for characters and plots. She wrote in black ink on blue paper,
crossing out and correcting as she went. When her words became too
messy to read, she pasted clean blue paper strips over the cross-outs,
sometimes four layers deep. As she finished pages, she would let them
flutter to the floor beside her bed, where a typist gathered them up.
After they were typed, Edith made more corrections. The same page
might be retyped as many as ten times.

Edith had signed a contract with Scribner's to do another long
novel, which would first appear, chapter by chapter, in *Scribner's Magazine.* She was having trouble settling down to work on it until a letter
from Mr. Burlingame in August 1904 jolted her into action. A book by
another author, scheduled to begin appearing in the magazine before
Edith's, was not ready. Could Edith have the first chapters of her novel
finished by January 1905 and provide the rest of the book, chapter by
chapter, over the next few months?

Edith called this proposal "the severest test to which a novelist can
be subjected." The public would begin reading her novel in the issues
of *Scribner's Magazine* before she had figured out how it would end. It
wasn't that she didn't know what the conclusion would be. "My last page
is always latent in my first," she claimed. "But the intervening wind-
ings of the way become clear only as I write, and now I was asked to gal-
lop over them before I had even traced them out!" When Mr.

Burlingame pressed her for an answer, she responded with the most courageous and important "yes" of her writing career.

And then she set to work. Anna Bahlmann (first her governess, then her secretary, now her literary assistant) was a tremendous help just when Edith needed it most. There would be no thought, this time, of losing her nerve or her confidence, as when she had dithered around with her first book of short stories ten years earlier. There would be no wailing letters about bad health, no pushing back of deadlines. Each deadline would be met, each chapter would reach her editor's desk on time.

By spring, it was obvious that the public was seriously hooked on Edith's story. People were used to seeing her short pieces in various magazines, but her novel, published in installments, several chapters per issue, was a sensation. Readers lined up at newsstands to buy the latest copy of *Scribner's Magazine* and find out what would happen to Edith's twenty-nine-year-old heroine, Lily Bart. Lily's love interest, Lawrence Selden, was, as Edith told Sally Norton, a "negative hero," a man who could talk but lacked the ability to act. By fall, both Edith and her readers knew how it all came out.

When *The House of Mirth* was published in book form in October 1905, it was the fastest-selling volume ever published by Scribner's. Within two months it was at the top of the bestseller list. Readers wrote to say they were crushed over Lily Bart's death in the second-to-last chapter. Couldn't Lily and the hero, Lawrence Selden,

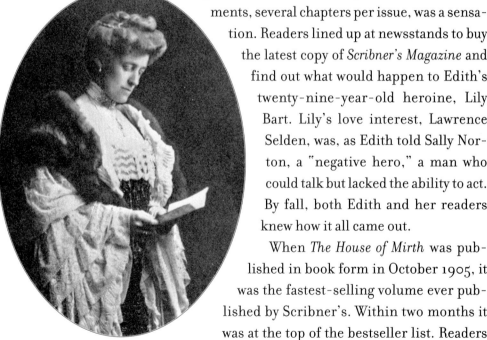

• • •

Edith in December 1905: elegant society woman and best-selling novelist.

(one line.)

Lily took no sleeping-drops that night. She lay
awake thinking of her situation, in
the crude light which Rosedale's visit
had projected on it. She was beginning to
think that in rejecting the offer
he was so plainly ready to renew, she
had she not sacrificed to one of those abstract
notions of honour that might be called
the conventionalities of the moral life.?
She owed no debt What debt did she
owe to a social order which had condemned
& banished her without trial? She had
never been heard in her own defence; & she
was innocent of the charge on which she
had been convicted; & the irregularity of
her the methods used in proving her
might seem to justify her the use of
methods equally irregular in recovering
her lost rights. Bertha Dorset, to save

• • •

A handwritten page from Book II of The House of Mirth, *with numerous corrections and jagged
right and left edges where strips have been pasted.*

have gotten together? Edith was so "persecuted" by mail that she asked her editors to stop giving out her address. Out for a walk in Lenox late in the fall of 1905, Edith was confronted by an indignant woman. "I have just finished reading *The House of Mirth*," she said. "It was bad enough that you had the heart to kill Lily. But here you are, shamelessly parading the streets in a red hat!"

An old friend of Edith's stayed up late into the night to finish the novel. "It is a very remarkable book," he wrote to his wife. "New York Society as it really is, as one really knows it, has never been written about before. . . . One knows all the people without being able to name one of them. Save I think Walter Berry is the hero." One reader claimed Edith had "stripped" New York society in her novel. "New York society is still amply clad," Edith responded, "& the little corner of its garment that I lifted was meant to show only . . . the group of idle & dull people . . . that exists in any big & wealthy social body. . . . Forgive this long discourse—but you see I had to come to the defense of my own town."

Despite her passionate defense of her New York, Europe was pulling at Edith's heart. On March 1, 1906, Edith wrote to Sally Norton: "We are sailing on the 10th—for Paris first, & then for six weeks in England. . . . I am going chiefly for a rest & . . . mental refreshment. . . . Oh the curse of having been brought up there, & having it ineradically [*sic*] in one's blood!"

She arrived in Paris a celebrity, the fa-

. . .

Shown here in France in the early 1900s, Edith was more and more drawn toward what eventually became her adopted country.

mous author of *The House of Mirth*. In New York, high society looked down on artists and intellectuals. In France, to Edith's great delight, artists, intellectuals, politicians, and the nobility mingled easily at salons, regular gatherings that took place in the drawing rooms of certain upper-class homes. The salons of Paris were, in Edith's opinion, "the best school of talk and of ideas that the modern world has known." Edith's French friend Paul Bourget was more than willing to escort her to the best of them. The most important salon he took her to was hosted by the Comtesse Robert de Fitz-James—Rosa to her friends.

. . .

Henry James in 1905, just before his second visit to the Mount. On this visit, through after-dinner chats on the veranda and long drives through the Lenox countryside, he and Edith became close friends. Photograph by Katherine McClellen; courtesy of Smith College Archives, Smith College.

Rosa, a widow, was a "small thin woman . . . perhaps forty-five years old" who was "always eager to welcome any foreigners likely to fit into the carefully-adjusted design of her *salon*, which, at that time, was the meeting-place of some of the most distinguished people in Paris." Rosa was not herself an intellectual. Her gift was providing a place for intellectuals to gather. Edith called her "a book-collector, not a reader. . . . Her books were an ornament and an investment; she never pretended that they were anything else." Rosa dutifully bought the latest book by each of her distinguished guests, tried (usually unsuccessfully) to read it, then whispered to someone else in her circle: "I've just read So-and-So's new book. *Tell me, my dear: is it good?*"

While Edith was getting to know fascinating people in Paris, Teddy (who didn't speak French and found intellectual conversation trying) popped over to London to buy a secondhand automobile. At the end of April, Edith joined him. She and Teddy and Cook and their newly bought automobile took Henry James on a short motor trip through

England. Cook, who had learned to deal with Edith's "help," now had to endure Henry James's as well: "This—this, my dear Cook, yes . . . this certainly is the right corner. But no; stay! A moment longer, please—in this light it's so difficult . . . appearances are so misleading. . . . It may be . . . yes! I think it *is* the next turn . . . 'a little farther lend thy guiding hand' . . . that is, drive on; but slowly, please, my dear Cook; *very* slowly!" When Henry stopped to ask directions, he was equally confusing. "In short my good man," he said to one astonished local, "what I want to put to you in a word is this: supposing we have already (as I have reason to think we have) driven past the turn down to the railway station (which, in that case, by the way, would probably not have been on our left hand, but on our right), where are we now in relation to . . ." And on he rambled, never thinking to mention where it was they were trying to go.

The trip ended with a stop to visit Henry's friend Howard Sturgis at his home, called Queen's Acre. It was one of the most delightful gathering places Edith was ever to encounter, and she visited it often over the years. Howard Sturgis was a man of means with a "reluc-

• • •

Queen's Acre, Howard Sturgis's home in Windsor, England.

tance to repair, to repaint or in any way renovate his dear old house." Outside Queen's Acre was a "weedy lawn . . . a shrubbery edged with an unsuccessful herbaceous border" and a "not too successful rose garden." Behind the shrubbery there was said to be a coach, a coachman, and some aged horses, but they never seemed to appear. Visitors were better off arranging their own transportation.

Inside Queen's Acre there were neither electric lights nor telephones nor central heating. But there was a drawing room with "white-panelled walls hung with water-colours of varying merit" and "profound chintz arm-chairs drawn up about a hearth on which a fire always smouldered." And there was Howard Sturgis, the "drollest, kindest and strangest of men," stretched out on a "lounge," shawl over his legs, hands busy with knitting needles or embroidery. He was "indolent and unambitious," but "his social gifts were irresistible, and his drawing-room . . . was always full of visitors."

One of his frequent visitors (besides, of course, Edith and Henry) was Percy Lubbock. Percy, in his late twenties, was the youngest of Edith's bachelor friends. Perhaps because he was young and a bit in awe of Henry James and Edith Wharton, he found his place "in the shade" of the Queen's Acre gatherings, watching and listening. What he heard in those conversations was "like a sort of concerto, a concourse of instruments supporting the guest of honour. Henry James accompanied her with the whole weight of his orchestra. Howard Sturgis joined in with his nimble descant, so deceptively simple." Percy observed that "here, in such talk, she let herself go; here was freedom and breathable air." In his estimation, "the game of conversation delighted her, and she was a match for the best in it."

Another frequent visitor to Queen's Acre was an American transplant named Gaillard Lapsley, an acquaintance of Edith's who'd left the United States to teach at Cambridge University in England. He knew Edith differently from all the other Queen's Acre visitors. To Percy

• • •

Howard Sturgis (left) at Queen's Acre with a houseguest.

Lubbock and the others, Edith was a "meteor from overseas." Gaillard
Lapsley, on the other hand, had an "old and easy acquaintance" with
Edith. He had known her "at home . . . in her native air . . . quietly and
privately" and "he seemed, even before he admired and applauded her,
to be fond of her."

In Edith's 1902 novel, *The Valley of Decision*, her heroine searches in
vain for "an answering mind," much as Edith had for so many years. By

1906, at age forty-four, Edith finally found what she was looking for. She gathered her bachelors (Henry James, Howard Sturgis, Gaillard Lapsley, and Percy Lubbock) on one side of the English Channel and a group of French intellectuals, including Paul Bourget and others who frequented Rosa's salon, on the other. Back in the United States, there were her more recent acquaintances Sally Norton and her father, along with Edith's old friends Egerton Winthrop and Walter Berry. Out of the intellectual isolation of her young years she had formed what her *House of Mirth* hero Lawrence Selden called "a republic of the spirit." She had escaped from shallow society people, whose talk was limited to the next social event and problems with the servants, into a world of good company and stimulating conversation.

But even a citizen of the republic of the spirit needs to live somewhere. Edith was seriously wondering where she belonged . . . where her heart lay. Was it in the country of her birth? Or was it somewhere in Europe?

· SEVEN ·

Wych-hazel

No one had ever known she had a lover.
No one—of that she was absolutely sure.

"Atrophy," short story, 1927

For the present, Edith wanted both America and Europe, and she swung back and forth across the Atlantic every year. After each summer at the Mount, Edith heard France calling her, more and more insistently. Though Teddy didn't hear that call, he dutifully sailed back across the ocean with Edith. "The great and glorious pendulum," Henry called her.

The trip to France following the summer of 1906 was more than a visit. This time around, Edith and Teddy brought along two dogs and six servants and sublet an apartment, number 58 rue de Varenne, from the George Vanderbilts. Everyone took French lessons, and Cook, the chauffeur, began navigating the roads both in and outside Paris as if

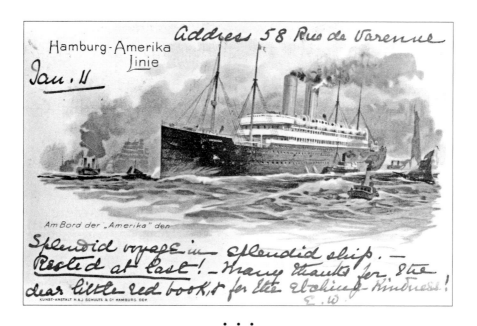

Hamburg-Amerika Linie

Address 58 *Rue de Varenne*

Jan. 11

Am Bord der „Amerika" den

Splendid voyage in splendid ship. — Rested at last! — Many thanks for the dear little red book, & for the etching — kindness!

E. W.

KUNST-ANSTALT H.&J SCHULTE & Cº HAMBURG. DEP.

• • •

Between 1885 and 1914, Edith crossed the Atlantic in both directions almost every year.
She didn't usually enjoy sea travel, but on this 1907 postcard to Sally Norton she wrote,
"Splendid voyage in splendid ship.—Rested at last!"

he'd driven them all his life. On January 24, 1907, Edith celebrated her forty-fifth birthday in their new apartment. "There was a curious strangeness in keeping a birthday in my own home, as it were, yet in a 'foreign' place," she wrote Sally.

For Edith, 58 rue de Varenne was perfect. It was in the part of Paris called Faubourg St. Germain, where family properties had been handed down for generations and strict rules were observed: No hanging out the wash or shaking carpets out the windows. No loud noises. Only well-behaved animals, like Edith's dogs, were permitted. These were not arbitrary rules but sensible ones, which made number 58 a quiet, civilized island in the middle of the wonderful, exploding life of Paris. Number 58 was two blocks away from Paul and Minnie Bourget's home and just around the corner from the salon of Rosa de Fitz-James.

And what a friend Rosa turned out to be. "I soon became an

Number 58 rue de Varenne, photographed around 1969.
It looked much the same in Edith's day.

habitual guest at her weekly lunches and dinners," Edith remembered. Rosa put her dinner parties together with scrupulous care. She avoided inviting "two champions likely to talk each other down," and she took seriously the unwritten rule that a good hostess should "never go out—*never*—if she expects people to come to her."

Edith put together her own salon at 58 rue de Varenne. Paul Bourget dropped in from around the corner. Henry James, Howard Sturgis, Percy Lubbock, and Gaillard Lapsley dropped in from England. Walter Berry and Egerton Winthrop dropped in from America. Edith never let distance interfere; she and her circle of male friends gathered as easily and as regularly as if they all lived in the same small neighborhood.

Edith certainly didn't obey the rule about a hostess never going out. In fact, she went out so much that Henry James was deeply concerned about what would happen to him when he crossed the channel for a visit. Henry James's writing life was very different from Edith's. He withdrew from the world to create his novels. He needed large stretches of quiet and the familiar walls of Lamb House to do his work. When he thought of his very settled existence and then looked ahead to a planned trip across the channel to visit Edith and

Teddy, he wrote to a friend, "I know I shall (inevitably) be involved in the movements, the general rhythmic rush of my host and hostess—the latter especially—to say nothing (alas!) of that of their automobile; and they probably have plans."

And of course, Edith did have plans. As soon as Henry arrived, she and Teddy swept him away in their automobile, named George (the replacement for a previous automobile named Alfred), for a tour of southern France . . . and Henry loved it. When he wrote to Howard Sturgis, he had completely changed his tune: "My three weeks of really seeing this large incomparable France in our friend's chariot of fire has been almost the time of my life. It's the old travelling carriage way glorified and raised to the 100th power."

During her 1907 stay at 58 rue de Varenne, Edith added yet one more bachelor to her collection, a dapper, dark-haired, blue-eyed fellow named William Morton Fullerton whom she'd met at Rosa's salon. He was an American expatriate living in Paris who had offered to help her arrange the serialization of *The House of Mirth* in a French magazine and was taking so much trouble with it that Edith finally invited him to be her houseguest. He was also a friend of Sally Norton's. In April 1907, Edith wrote to Sally that she found Morton Fullerton "very intelligent, but slightly mysterious, I think." She learned that he was planning to visit his relatives in America, so just before she left Europe for the summer, she let him know she was "find-able at 'The Mount, Lenox, Mass'" until Christmas. Henry James warned her not to count on a visit from Morton, as he wasn't the most dependable of people.

But in late October, Morton arrived at the Mount. An early snowfall had dusted the countryside, and Edith took him on an idyllic drive through the Berkshires. While Cook stopped the car to put chains on the tires, Edith and Morton sat by the road and picked two sprigs from a witch hazel shrub. After Morton left the Mount to return to his job in Paris as a correspondent for the London *Times*, he sent Edith a thank-you note with his witch hazel sprig tucked inside, and Edith began a secret journal written to an unnamed "you." She titled it "L'Ame Close" ("The Life Apart" or "The Shut-Off Soul"); scholars refer to it as the Love Diary. The beloved "you" in the journal was Morton Fullerton. "If you had not enclosed that sprig of wych-hazel in your note I should not have opened this long-abandoned book," she wrote. "But now I shall have the illusion that I am talking to you." At age forty-five, she found special significance in the witch hazel, sometimes referred to as the old woman's flower, because it blooms in the autumn. Edith Wharton, the moral, aloof chronicler of society affairs, was feeling a late-blooming passion in her own heart. Perhaps believing she could enjoy this forbidden attraction without acting on it, she recorded her feelings in the Love Diary and tried to treat Morton as she did her other bachelor friends.

A few days after Morton left for Paris, Edith decided the Mount was getting too chilly to live in and pushed the Whartons' own departure for Paris up to December 5. As soon as she set foot in France, she felt her energy stir. Teddy, on the other hand, collapsed in a nervous depression very much like the one he'd suffered four years earlier. As Teddy retreated into his mysterious illness, Morton became a frequent visitor to number 58.

Edith persuaded Teddy that it might lift his spirits if he got away from Paris and went to see some friends. She said goodbye to him at the train station and promptly took off on a series of motor tours with Morton. In a church they visited, she found her way to a shadowy corner where she imagined a veiled figure that "stole up & looked at me a moment." Writing about the incident in her secret Love Diary, she wondered, "Was its name Happiness?" Later, Morton visited her apartment and said something that caused her to write, "You hurt me—you disillusioned me—& when you left me I was more deeply yours."

Teddy suddenly returned, but he was feeling no better. Now, Edith

• • •

The Mount after a snowfall.

wrote Sally, he was complaining of awful pains in his head. In March, Edith put Teddy on a ship to America so he could go to Hot Springs, Arkansas, for a treatment. She resumed her motor trips with Morton. In the daily letters they exchanged between trips, Edith dared to be more open about her feelings. "I have found in Emerson . . . just the phrase for you—& *me.* 'The moment my eyes fell on him I was content,'" she wrote in one letter; and in another, "I'm so afraid that the treasures I long to unpack for you . . . *are* only, to you, the old familiar red calico & beads." Would Morton think these "treasures" were

· · ·

Edith at age forty-five, right around the time she first met Morton Fullerton. Six years earlier, she had written a short story titled "Copy," a dialogue between two famous writers and former lovers worried about how each might misuse the other's letters. The story uncannily predicted the situation in which Edith found herself later on.

intellectual thoughts or something more?

The sublet on the Vanderbilts' apartment was up, but Edith couldn't bear to leave France, so she moved into her brother Harry's Paris townhouse. She and Morton stole every opportunity to be together, either alone or in company. They were now exchanging kisses and caresses whenever they could. The relationship was conducted in secret; husband, friends, and the ever-present servants must not suspect what was going on.

Finally, it was time for Edith to go. The night before her May departure, proper, reserved Edith Wharton took a bold step: She gave Morton her Love Diary to read, revealing to him that she'd fallen in love with him on his visit to the Mount. He returned the diary the next morning when he accompanied her to the train station.

That wretched train, and then an even more wretched ship, took her away from the city and the man she was infatuated with, to an isolated country home and a sick, unhappy husband. She settled in at the Mount—miserably. Morton wrote her three letters, then two more, and then there was silence. He was not singling her out for insensitive treatment. This was exactly how he behaved toward all the women in his life, and though Edith didn't know it at the time, there were many: a former wife, current and former mistresses, and a young woman he was engaged to but had no intention of marrying.

Edith wrote to Henry James asking about Morton. She hadn't heard from their mutual friend in a while and wondered if he was all right. It was as far as she could go on that subject. She also wrote Henry about Teddy's endless depressions and ailments, which the doctors couldn't find a cause for and which were almost more than she could endure. "I am deeply distressed at the situation you describe," Henry replied from England. "Only sit tight yourself and *go through the movements of life*. . . . Believe meanwhile and always in the aboundingly tender friendship— the understanding, the participation, the *princely* (though I say it who shouldn't) hospitality of spirit and soul of yours more than ever, Henry James."

Edith's return passage to Europe was booked for October 30—weeks earlier than usual—and Teddy wouldn't be joining her until January. Walter Berry had been appointed to a judgeship on the International Tribunal in Cairo, Egypt, and she would be making the voyage across the Atlantic with him. As soon as Walter and Edith arrived in London, Gaillard Lapsley, Henry James, and Howard Sturgis came into the city to join them. Surrounded by her bachelors, Edith toured and lunched and laughed. "I am sleeping better, & am very glad I came away, for the change & movement carry me along, help to form an *outer surface*," she wrote Sally.

The frenetic movement that was helping Edith was terrifying to Henry James. He could write encouraging things to Edith when distance (preferably a large body of water) separated them. But when she actually descended on England, it took all he could muster to protect himself. He described Edith's 1908 months in England as "general eagle-pounces & eagle-flights of her deranging & desolating, ravaging, burning & destroying energy." He referred to Edith as "the Angel of Devastation." The two huge unknowns in Edith's life—whether Morton still had feelings for her and the mysterious cause of Teddy's illness— seemed to increase her activity to a frantic level.

Edith wrote to Morton in a very businesslike tone, asking him to return her letters, if any of them survived. Morton replied, "The letters survive, & everything survives," which left her thoroughly confused. So she continued to move around England, adding two more bachelors to her collection: a handsome forty-year-old landscape painter named Robert Norton (no relation to Sally) and a twenty-seven-year-old banker named John Hugh-Smith.

When she crossed over to Paris, subletting number 58 rue de Varenne once more, Edith finally saw Morton again. His lack of communication, he explained, was due to a former mistress who was threatening to make certain letters public if he didn't pay her a sum of money she claimed he owed her. Edith took heart from the fact that the woman was a *former* mistress and assumed the role of problem solver. Morton welcomed her friendly help and, at the same time, kept her romantically attached to him by alternately wooing and ignoring her.

And then Teddy descended on number 58. The treatment he'd taken in Arkansas hadn't helped him at all, and he was in terrible shape. He couldn't sleep. His arms hurt, his legs hurt . . . even his face hurt. Gout was the diagnosis Edith had been clinging to, but now she began to suspect that whatever had hold of him was something else.

In mid-April 1909, Teddy sailed home to the Mount—without Edith. She had decided to skip America that year. Her year's lease on number 58 was up, so she moved into the Hotel Crillon. It was a relief to have Teddy gone, but almost immediately, bad news came from his physi-

• • •

*Morton Fullerton. Edith asked him several times to return
the love letters she had written him, but he never did.*

cian in Lenox. Dr. Francis Kinnicutt was sure Teddy's condition was not physical. It was his mind that was going. His moods swung with no warning from deep depressions, when he couldn't seem to move, to wild activity, when he couldn't keep still. On top of everything else, his mother had died. How would he handle that?

According to Teddy's sister, Nannie, he was handling it "perfectly." Teddy "seems *perfectly* well and *perfectly* normal now," Nannie wrote. Dr. Kinnicutt was more careful. "I am not free from anxiety about him," he wrote Edith. "My fear is that on his return to Paris, in an environment which does not appeal to him apart from the helpfulness of your presence, there may be another swing back of the pendulum." So Teddy stayed on in America, while Edith remained in Europe.

On June 1, Edith left Paris in her current automobile, which she had decided to name Hortense, with Morton sitting beside her in the back seat. Cook drove, and Gross, wearing her bonnet, sat beside him. They motored to the English Channel, endured a stormy crossing, and, arriving in London several days later, checked into a drab railway hotel called the Charing Cross. Morton would be setting out the next morning by train and then by ship to visit his family in the United States. Edith told Gross she would not need her that evening, and Edith and Morton retired to their suite, two separate bedrooms with an adjoining sitting room. This may not have been the first night Edith and Morton spent together, but it was by far the most memorable. Edith described it in a poem: "Wonderful was the long secret night you gave me, my Lover." Edith, who had always been so picky about her hotels, seemed to treasure "the low wide bed, as rutted and worn as a high-road" because it put her, finally, in the company of the commoners she envied for having experienced the passion she had missed all her life. The poem was called "Terminus," meaning endpoint, and it finished on a depressing note. The man goes out to "the wide flair of cities, with windy garlands and shouting," while the woman goes only to "a harbourless wind-bitten shore, where a dull town moulders and shrinks/And its roofs fall in."

Morton departed for America but was back in England by mid-July. He and Henry and Edith embarked on a week-long motor tour. This rapturous week was probably the "terminus" of the physical part of Edith Wharton's relationship to Morton Fullerton.

When they returned to France, Edith wrote him, "It is impossible . . . that our lives should run parallel much longer. I have faced the fact, & accepted it, & I am not afraid." She continued to be strongly attracted to him, but she couldn't risk her reputation on a long-term affair. Even if Morton had been inclined to consider marriage (and he wasn't), Edith was not willing to divorce Teddy. She had escaped from the part of society that frowned on her writing, but she had not left society itself. Stifling notions, like the idea that women mustn't write novels, should be thrown out; venerable old traditions, like marriage, must be carried on. Even if her own marriage was not what it should be, the institution itself was worth respecting. From here on in, she wanted to be Morton's soulmate, not his mistress.

With a great effort of will, Edith managed to slip Morton Fullerton back into her stable of bachelors, where she concluded he belonged. Her heart was not quick to accept her mind's decision, and Morton was only too willing to tempt her from time to time. Eventually, though, Edith's heart and mind were in agreement: Morton Fullerton would be a close friend with whom she shared a secret history. But he would be nothing more.

In 1909, just as she was struggling to put her relationship with Morton on a proper footing, an art critic named Bernard Berenson joined Edith's circle. Like Paul Bourget, Bernard was a married man. In dealing with her married men friends, Edith had to figure out how to handle their wives. She had close women friends, like Rosa and Sally and her sister-in-law, Minnie Jones. But Edith freely admitted that she didn't like the women attached to her male friends because she wanted undivided attention from their husbands. She had a particularly difficult time with Bernard Berenson's

• • •

Bernard Berenson. He and Edith traveled together, but there was never anything romantic between them. Perhaps as a reminder that Bernard had a wife at home, Mary Berenson gave Edith this photo on which she wrote: "To Edith—from Mary; BB as I first knew and adored him."

wife, Mary, especially as Bernard grew to a place in her affections second only to that of Walter Berry.

All socializing ground to a halt when Teddy and his sister, Nannie, arrived in Paris. On December 8, 1909, over dinner at the Crillon Hotel, Teddy dropped a bombshell: He confessed that he had rented an apartment in Boston and had kept a mistress there. Considering her just-ended affair with Morton Fullerton, Edith would have been hypocritical to condemn her husband for this. But there was more to his story. Since he had no real income of his own, Teddy had supported his mistress with $50,000 (the equivalent of over a million dollars today) that he had taken from Edith's trust fund. Edith had argued long and hard to have Teddy replace her adulterous brother Freddy as trustee of her fortune, and now Teddy had stolen from her in order to have an affair. His confession must have seemed like a cruel joke. The solution to it all must have seemed just as cruel to Teddy: Now that he had finally inherited some money of his own after his mother's death, most of it would be spent repaying his debt to his wife's estate.

Teddy sailed to America just before Christmas to set about making things right. Edith moved into a new rented apartment her brother had found for her right across the street from number 58. Number 53 rue de Varenne was not a sublet; it was hers all year round. So Edith wouldn't have to worry about moving out each summer. It would be her home in Paris for the next nine years.

When her ailing husband returned from the United States and joined her there, it marked the beginning of the most depressing years of Edith's life. All her activities and all her thoughts turned upon one single dilemma: What to do about Teddy.

EIGHT

Storm and Sorrow

It was one thing to theorize on the detachability of human beings,
another to watch them torn apart by the bleeding roots.

Twilight Sleep, *1927*

dith's husband was impossible to live with. His moods swung
from nervous excitement to gloom to rage. Although both Teddy's sister, Nannie, and his brother, Billy, continued to insist Teddy was perfectly reasonable, a physician friend in Paris advised Edith not to be
alone with him unless someone were near enough to hear if she called
for help. Still, according to the doctors, Teddy's condition was not yet
grave enough to justify committing him to an institution. "And if you
knew, if you *knew*, what the days are, what the hours are, what our talks
are," Edith wrote to Morton. "What is killing me is doing him no good!"

Morton was of little help. Often he didn't even answer her letters.
But Walter Berry arrived like a white knight to the rescue. He had

resigned his post in Egypt and wanted to settle down in Paris. While he was looking for his own place, he moved in with Edith and Teddy for a six-month stay. For Edith, just to have someone to talk to was a relief.

Perhaps a trip around the world would be good for Teddy. Edith put her husband on a ship with a helpful friend and hoped for the best. But when the voyage ended six months later, he was no better. He took off on a fishing trip with his brother, and Edith promised she would be waiting for him at the Mount when he returned. On June 24, 1911, she boarded a ship bound for America and what Henry James assumed would be "the storm and sorrow of the last act of your personal drama."

At the Mount she busied herself with the gardens she hadn't seen for two summers. And she waited for Teddy. Three friends—Henry James, John Hugh-Smith, and Gaillard Lapsley—came for a few days to shore her up for whatever Teddy's arrival might bring.

Edith in a fur-trimmed coat and hat, photographed by Peter Powel around 1910.

Henry James decided the stifling heat was a threat to his very life. Trying to keep him cool provided some comic moments, which eased the tension Edith was feeling. "Electric fans, iced drinks and cold baths seemed to give no relief; and finally we discovered that the only panacea was incessant motoring." So, with Cook at the wheel, they motored . . . and motored some more. They tried stopping for tea. Edith suggested that John Hugh-Smith read aloud one of Henry's favorite poems. But it turned out to be a long poem, and Henry immediately began to wilt. So it was back into the car and "off again on the incessant quest for air."

Gaillard Lapsley and John Hugh-Smith left, and Edith suggested that, in view of

Henry's misery, he move his departure date up a day. With an electric fan clutched in his hand and a pile of sucked oranges beside him, he fumed, "Good God, what a woman—what a woman! Her imagination boggles at nothing! She does not even scruple to project me in naked flight across the Atlantic." He would stay till his appointed departure date. Besides, now that he was alone with Edith, he had some serious advice for her: She should sell the Mount and separate from Teddy. It was the only reasonable thing to do. It was not the kind of advice Edith was ready to hear. Her sense of what was right and proper had been formed in the religious, dutiful Old New York of her childhood. The excesses of the Gilded Age, when couples divorced and remarried without a thought, didn't shake her conviction that marriage, even a poor, fractured one like hers, was the very foundation

Silver haired and still handsome, Walter Berry posed on the railing of the veranda during a quick visit to the Mount in the summer of 1911.

of a decent society. Divorce was a threat to the order and stability of civilization itself. She would not hear of it. She would find another way to deal with the Teddy problem.

When Teddy finally appeared, Henry was stunned at the change in the man he once knew. Teddy was "utterly quarrelsome, abusive, perpetual-scene-making & impossible," he wrote to Howard Sturgis. "He simply & absolutely . . . will do her to death."

Reluctantly, Henry left Edith to sort things out with her very disturbed husband. Edith's letters describing the weeks at the Mount following Henry's departure went from one extreme to another, probably in tandem with Teddy's mood swings. Things were "about as bad as they could be," she wrote to Minnie Jones. And to Gaillard Lapsley, "Teddy looks splendidly, and is really much better in every way." Those weeks were not, as Henry had predicted, the last act in the drama of the Wharton marriage. The final act was yet to come.

At the end of that distressing summer of 1911, Teddy headed to French Lick, Indiana, for a treatment, and Edith sailed for Europe. No decision had been made about the Mount or about the state of their marriage. Edith did sign papers giving Teddy authority to sell their Lenox home if he chose, but she expected him to let her know what he had decided before taking action. What to do with the Mount was a question that loomed as large as the Teddy question in Edith's mind. She'd sold her home in New York two years earlier. Selling the Mount would cut her last tie with America. She would be left with one home, and that home would be her rented apartment at number 53 rue de Varenne in Paris. Could she leave America for good? By the time she reached Europe, the question was answered. Teddy cabled that he had sold the Mount. The decision had been made.

A few weeks after her Atlantic crossing, Edith's sixteenth book was published. It was a novella called *Ethan Frome*, and it came as a complete shock to her readers. It was not about high society. It was set in one of the lonely, isolated Massachusetts towns she had seen on drives around the Mount, and its plot was bleak and hopeless. In trying to escape from a loveless marriage, the hero unintentionally turns the beautiful young woman he loves into an ugly, spiteful invalid. And it is Ethan himself who must care for both his dour wife and the creature his young love has become. "There was no way out—none," Ethan thinks. "He was a prisoner for life." The critics called it a "cruel story," but they couldn't deny that *Ethan Frome* was a masterpiece, "something very much finer

• • •

The library at the Mount. Edith and her guests spent many hours here talking or reading aloud.

and stronger" than anything Edith had written before. What readers and critics didn't guess was how autobiographical *Ethan Frome* was. It was a picture of Edith's own situation translated into fiction. Like Ethan, she was married to an invalid and trapped with no way out.

Though they were both avoiding it, Teddy and Edith knew they had to meet and talk sooner or later. Something had to be decided about their life as a married couple. In mid-December, Edith sent Teddy's butler, Alfred White, back to the United States to escort him to Paris.

Teddy arrived at number 53 in February 1912. Walter Berry had found his own place in Paris, but he now moved into Edith's guest suite to act as "shock-absorber." Edith hoped Teddy would take a trip south so that she could work on her current novel, *The Reef.* Instead, he settled into the apartment and begged Edith to help him learn French. Edith poured out her heart in a letter to Morton: "'Learning French' has become an obsession (*why?* that is so strange!), & we have been having a 'lesson,' & he has been crying, & saying over & over again: 'My mind is going, & the Drs don't see it.'—It seems to me that he is failing *very* fast mentally. It is too terrible!" He refused to leave the house unless Edith went with him. And all the while, she wrote Bernard Berenson, the unfinished manuscript of *The Reef* was "wailing for me every morning like an infant for the bottle."

• • •

French Lick Resort was one of the many places Teddy went in search of a cure for his mysterious disease.
In this 1915 photo of Pluto Spring, "Pluto" hosts the resort guests waiting to drink water from the
mineral spring, which supposedly had healing properties.

In May 1912, Teddy decided to sail back to New York. He and Edith had parted like this many times before. But this apparently routine leave-taking marked the last time they would ever be together as husband and wife. Without realizing it, they had just played out the final act of their marriage.

Edith turned—at last—back to writing *The Reef*. Morton was now the European representative of a publisher called D. Appleton, a company that offered Edith a higher advance than Scribner's ever had. Not yet ready to divorce her husband, she "divorced" her publisher and accepted Appleton's offer. "Mr. Scribner . . . is mortally hurt by my infidelity!" she told Morton.

But neither company would be publishing the book until it was finished. Still drawn to Morton, Edith was depending on him, rather than Walter, to help her complete it. Her letters pursued him: "Do you think you could perhaps come & see me somewhere for a day or two next month, so that I cd go over the Reef with you?" Two months later, she wrote: "I count on you for dinner tomorrow . . . drop a line in the morning to Appleton, to say that the End of 'The Reef' will go to them *positively* this week. . . . I shan't send the chapters till I've read them to you." There was a reason why Edith sought out Morton's comments rather than Walter's. *The Reef* was her first real love story, and only Morton would recognize the main characters—Anna Leath, a widow, and George Darrow, an older bachelor who wants to marry her—as fictionalized recreations of himself and Edith. Always the truth teller, Edith used *The Reef* to expose the weaknesses of both her hero and her heroine. Anna is insecure and puts Darrow off more than once even though she knows she loves him. Because Anna has left him hanging, Darrow gets caught up in a brief affair with a much younger woman, who later becomes engaged to Anna's grown son. If the book is a picture of Edith's relationship to Morton, she seems to be blaming herself, at least in part, for Morton's womanizing.

ETHAN FROME

Dramatized from the novel by

EDITH WHARTON

by

OWEN and DONALD DAVIS

▼

"The best theatrical statement that has yet been made of any of her novels." *John Mason Brown in The New York Evening Post*

"Beautiful beyond any cavil or misgiving." *Gilbert Gabriel in The New York American*

"What was essential to Edith Wharton's 'Ethan Frome'— the simplicity, the almost overpowering poignancy — is retained in the stage version . . . and the result is a tragedy which is deeply stirring and rather grimly beautiful." *Richard Lockridge in The New York Sun*

"Edith Wharton's story proves one of the finest of American plays. When a quarter of a century ago, Edith Wharton signed her distinguished name to 'Ethan Frome' it was immediately recognized as one of the finest American novels. Now, in the dramatization by Owen and Donald Davis, it is one of the finest American plays." *Robert Garland in The New York World Telegram*

"The best dramatization of a novel I have ever seen in a theatre." *John Anderson in The New York Evening Journal*

▲

Published by **CHARLES SCRIBNER'S SONS**

ETHAN FROME

A Dramatization of

EDITH WHARTON'S *Novel*

by OWEN DAVIS AND DONALD DAVIS

Scribners

• • •

Dust jacket from the dramatized version of Ethan Frome. *The play opened in 1936, twenty-five years after the novel was published, to high critical acclaim.*

Finally, she finished the novel and was "out of *its* clutches." Henry James found it superb. He thought it was "quite the finest thing" she had done. But the reviews were negative and the sales were terrible. Edith sent a copy to Bernard Berenson with a note: "Only *please* don't read it! Put it in the visitors' rooms, or lend it to somebody to read in the train & let it get lost."

Edith counted on her writing to take her away from her domestic misery. But this time, her writing had let her down. "If only my work were better," she wrote John Hugh-Smith, "it would be all I need! But my kind of half-talent isn't much use as an escape—at least more than temporarily."

A ten-day New Year's visit from Percy Lubbock and Gaillard Lapsley gave her some relief before the next blow. It came not from Teddy but from her brother Harry, who, according to Edith, was "under the rule of the woman he lives with." Harry resented the fact that Edith hadn't asked to meet her prospective sister-in-law. The woman called herself Countess Tekla, but no one could figure out if her title was legitimate. As it turned out, she and Harry didn't marry for another seven years. But the countess insisted that Harry break off communication with his sister and that he cut both Edith and his adopted daughter, Beatrix, out of his will.

Harry had found Edith's Paris apartment for her, had traveled with her, had been "the dearest of brothers to all my youth." And now he wouldn't even talk to her. Edith was devastated.

In the wake of her "divorce" from Scribner's and her brother's "divorce" from her, Edith reconsidered her relationship to Teddy. It was no longer a marriage in any true sense of the word and it was making them both miserable. Teddy's sister consistently blocked any move to have Teddy committed, but she left his care up to Edith. It made for an impossible situation. Edith decided it was time to divorce Teddy. Nannie (who still insisted her brother was perfectly fine) could take over. Edith set the legal wheels in motion and then she waited . . . and waited. She and Walter were on a trip to Sicily just before Easter when Teddy appeared in Paris and was served the divorce papers. Twenty-four hours later, on April 16, 1913, it was final. Edith was fifty-one years old. She and Teddy had been married for almost twenty-eight years, and it was over. She was a divorced woman.

Teddy was belligerent. He was "damned well rid of her." He spread rumors accusing his former wife of having "improper relations with Walter Berry and several others." They were scooped up by newspapers on both sides of the Atlantic. For once, Ogden Codman's contribution to the gossip was useful. Edith didn't have the temperament for anything as passionate as an affair, he sniffed. And besides, Walter Berry was so "anemic" that he wouldn't be of "much use in a naughty way."

Edith was relieved that her ordeal was over. Now she felt the need to move, to do something with the energy that had built up inside her during all those months of waiting for the end of her marriage. So she dashed about from place to place, determined to eat the world "leaf by leaf." First she was off to England, where she was thinking of buying a house to replace the Mount. Percy Lubbock and Gaillard Lapsley went house hunting with her. She wouldn't buy just now, she decided. But she did arrange to rent a place in England for the following summer. Then she took a trip through Luxembourg and Germany with Bernard Berenson.

In October 1913, a novel she'd been working on in fits and starts for almost five years, *The Custom of the Country*, was finally published. The heroine, Undine Spragg, was a pitiless "swell" from Apex, Kansas, whose marriages and divorces moved her up the ladder to money, but not to social acceptability. In spite of the fact that Undine was thoroughly dislikable, critics gave the book excellent reviews and it sold steadily and well.

Edith Wharton was, by then, thought of as the most accomplished and admired American writer of the day. Her readers could usually count on a book a year from her. And while they waited for her next book, they could read her short stories in magazines like *Scribner's* or *Harper's* or the *Atlantic Monthly*.

The trip that ended the year 1913 took Edith across the Atlantic to New York City, where she gathered with friends and what was left of the Jones family. The occasion was the marriage of her forty-one-year-old niece, Beatrix.

Ogden Codman, also a guest at the wedding, pointed out to his mother that the Joneses were "rather down on their luck." Freddy Jones's divorce and second marriage to a "harlot," Harry's "unedifying condition with another ancient harlot," and now Edith's divorce "have made them rather forlorn." Beatrix was the only grandchild of George Frederic and Lucretia, and her marriage, so late in life, made the likelihood of her having children iffy at best.

Now that she was a "divorced woman," Edith was only too aware of how New York society might receive her. Of course Beatrix's mother, Minnie Jones, gave her a warm reception. Minnie was a long-time friend who knew firsthand what it was to be divorced. But what about the rest of New York? As it turned out, New Yorkers were a little *too* ready to welcome Edith, now that she was a famous writer. They made her feel as though she were being moved about like a pawn in some game. Mary Berenson, also visiting New York, thought Edith "spoiled several evenings especially arranged for her by evidently hating everything." Mary also thought Edith was "nervous with jealousy" because Walter Berry was rumored to be close to an engagement with a certain New York woman. He was pointedly *not* with Edith at many of the social events where she expected him to be her escort.

Edith decided to return to Paris earlier than she'd planned. And she decided Walter would sail with her. He told everyone how much he didn't want to go, but he went anyway. The marriage rumors about Walter and the New York woman faded away, which set everyone to wondering about Walter and Edith. Would they finally marry, now that Edith was single and available? According to Alfred White, the butler, who stayed with Edith after the divorce, marriage to Walter was not even remotely possible. In his opinion, Walter would have married at a younger age if he were inclined to marry at all, and he still enjoyed the attentions of all the younger women who surrounded him like flies.

Marriage to Walter may not have been what Edith wanted, either. Romance could damage a friendship between a man and a woman, and it was really Walter's friendship that she treasured. Perhaps in snatching Walter away from New York, she was protecting his bachelorhood rather than staking her own claim on him. And, as much as Walter might grumble, her favorite bachelor may have welcomed that protection. So Edith and Walter didn't marry. But they stayed the closest of friends.

On the voyage back to France, Edith took time to write a note to her newly married niece. "Fasten with all your might on the inestimable treasure of your liking for each other. . . . And if you have a boy or girl, to prolong the joy, so much the better. Be sure it's worthwhile. *And times come when one would give anything in the world for a reason like that for living on.*"

Her divorce, the break with her brother Harry, and her defection from Scribner's to Appleton had made 1913 a horrible year for Edith. She even had a nightmare about it. In her dream she saw "a pale demon" and "four black gnome-like creatures carrying a great black trunk." The demon cried out, "Here's your year—here are all the horrors that have happened to you," and he threw a bunch of "limp black squirming things" on the floor before her.

Edith hoped her next year would be a better one. It certainly started out to be. She began a new novel called *Literature,* which she hoped would be her "best and most comprehensive piece of work." She traveled to north Africa with Percy Lubbock. And she was looking forward to a trip to Spain with Walter in July. She was sure 1914 would be a good year.

But then she remembered the last little bit of the nightmare she'd had. When the demon had finished pulling all the black squirming events of 1913 out, she had stared at the empty trunk and asked him, *"Are you sure it hasn't a false bottom?"* Were there more demons, hiding in that trunk and ready to spring?

· NINE ·

The Worst of Doing Good

France, his France, attacked, invaded, outraged—and he, a poor helpless
American boy, who adored her, and could do nothing for her. . . . It was bitter.

The Marne, *1918*

It was early July 1914 when Edith and Walter set out on their motor tour of Spain. On the day they left Paris, there was some unsettling talk about an incident that had taken place in Sarajevo. Like most of her European friends, Edith wasn't entirely sure where Sarajevo was. The news that the Austrian archduke and his wife had been assassinated in that capital of Bosnia by a Serbian suddenly made this faraway place significant. Would Austria, which administered Bosnia, and Austria's ally Germany react to the assassination by attacking Serbia? Would Russia, Serbia's ally, then come to Serbia's defense? Would France, Russia's ally, then . . . ? Surely not. Most people were convinced that kings, presidents, and diplomats would do what they'd always done and take charge of the situation. The rumors of war were obviously just that: rumors. Edith and Walter "gave little thought to the poor murdered Archduke, and international politics seemed as remote as the moon."

Once they reached Spain, the "glorious hours of air & scenery" chased all concerns out of their minds. Edith's only complaint (and such a small one, considering all that lay just ahead) was of not having enough time to enjoy the sights because Walter pushed her faster than she wanted to go. "Spain in July is the most delicious place imaginable," she wrote to Bernard Berenson. "But how tell it in Spanish, or any other language when one tumbles out of the motor at 7 p.m. to leap into it again at 9?"

She and Walter crossed the border back into France on July 26, 1914. The international news was disturbing. Even so, they took their time getting to Paris. The weather and the scenery were too lovely. Surely nothing could disturb such peace and beauty. From a hotel room in the south of France, Edith heard crowds outside her window singing the French national anthem all night long. When she and Walter met for breakfast the next morning, they wondered about the possibility of war. But as they motored north, Edith felt reassured by the calm of the countryside. "The air seemed full of the long murmur of human effort, the rhythm of oft-repeated tasks."

She spent her first night back in Paris at the Hotel Crillon. She'd closed up number 53 before her trip with Walter, and her house staff was waiting for her at the country home she'd arranged to rent in England. In Paris, the "air was thundery with rumours." But arguing against those "rumours" was the "whole incalculable weight of things-as-they-were."

On August 2, 1914, the faraway world of kings, presidents, and diplomats crashed rudely into the ordinary world of things-as-they-were. German soldiers were armed and on their way through Belgium. France mobilized for war. Where had it come from, this war? It felt like an ugly storm that had suddenly dropped out of a cloudless blue sky.

As Edith stood bewildered in the middle of Paris-grown-foreign, she recorded what mobilization looked like: "A huge break in the normal flow of traffic, like the sudden rupture of a dyke." People flooded down the streets on their way to railway stations. They were all on foot because there were no taxis to be had. "The War Office had thrown out its drag-net and caught them all in" to assist with military transportation. As for people like Edith, "the army of midsummer travel was immobilized to let the other army move. . . . No train stirred except to carry soldiers." There was the "resounding emptiness of porterless halls, waiterless restaurants, motionless lifts" and "the gradual paralysis of the city."

Now the war was in charge. But Edith could at least find a way to pitch in. First, America must know what was happening in Europe. "DETAINED IN PARIS EXTRAOR-

*A 1915 motor vehicle permit for Edith's car,
naming Walter Berry and Charles Cook as chauffeurs.*

DINARY SIGHTS DO YOU WANT IMPRESSIONS" she cabled her editor at *Scribner's Magazine.* When he replied, the first of a series of articles shot across the Atlantic.

Watching and writing about what she saw wasn't enough. Edith needed action. In a matter of days she'd found a task. Well-meaning rich women had turned their drawing rooms into hospitals, and some were making shirts for the wounded, robbing French seamstresses of their only way to make a living. The French Red Cross had a request. Could Mrs. Wharton raise enough funds to open a workroom and pay unemployed women to make bandages, socks, and sweaters? Edith had no idea how to go about such a thing. But "there was an ardour in the air which made it seem easy to accomplish what ever one attempted."

Yes, Mrs. Wharton, the writer and high-society woman, could open a workroom. She rolled up her silk sleeves. Within weeks she had talked her wealthy friends out of $2,000 (the equivalent of more than $40,000 today) and established a place where twenty seamstresses could earn a French franc a day and eat a hearty meal at noon. As soon as her workroom was up and running, she sailed over to England. Like her French friends, she believed the war would be over in a month or so, and she had done her bit.

She'd rented a country home thirty miles northwest of London, and it was just as "civilized & big-treed & gardened & library'd & pictured & garaged" as Henry James had described it. But in less than a week, she wrote to Sally Norton about how miserable she was there. "I hardly know with what feelings I sit down & write to you in this still & lonely place where I had dreamed of being so happy. . . . I left Paris only six days ago . . . & the very next day came the dreadful news of the German advance & the probable siege of Paris."

Things were desperate on the French side of the channel. "There began to be rumours of a big battle—*the* decisive battle." A million German soldiers had ripped a path through Belgium and were headed south toward Paris. On September 2, the French government fled to Bordeaux, and the woman in charge of Edith's workroom turned the workers out on the streets and left the city as well.

Edith, helpless in England, felt like a deserter. "My co-workers must think I had planned my flight," she wrote to Sally. And to Bernard Berenson, "I am simply sick & heart-broken at having left my workroom there at a time when I might have been of real use."

Having spent nearly three weeks trying to get to England, Edith now wanted to be in France, no matter what lay waiting for her there. The channel was blocked. France's fate hung in the balance as the French fought off a German attack sixty-five miles outside Paris. If the city fell, the war was lost. The military governor of Paris rallied a thousand city taxis to carry five thousand reinforcement troops to the battlefront at the Marne River.

Edith, and all of England, waited. Finally, word came from France: After a six-day battle, the Germans had been driven back across the Marne, and Paris was safe. That was the good news. The bad news was that the war would not end anytime soon. Huge armies—the French and their British allies on one side, the Germans and their Austrian allies on the other—had dug trenches and were settled in for a slow but deadly struggle that would last for who knew how long. But Paris was safe for the moment, and the channel was again open to travelers. Edith boarded a ferry bound for France.

The last time the Germans and French had fought was back in 1870, when Edith and her family were on their six-year tour of Europe. For the Joneses, that war was nothing more than a nuisance to be avoided, and the fact that France had been defeated was a small piece of bad luck. On September 14, 1914, Edith Wharton, now a woman of fifty-two, sailed across the English Channel into whatever the war would make of her life. France had helped her to escape from the stifling shallowness of New York society. Now she would cast her fate with France.

• • •

Edith transferred the business skills she'd learned in the literary world to the running
of her first war charity, a workroom for unemployed seamstresses and secretaries.

Soon after her return to Paris, she had her workroom up and running again. "We now have 50 women working there, & shall take more soon," she wrote Sally. "And all this keeps me busy & interested, so that I feel the oppression of the war much less than I did in England. . . . Paris is taking heart, people are coming back in thousands, there is more light in the streets, & I suppose soon a few more shops will open."

What she called "the blessed drug of hard work" would replace the joys of writing and reading and dining and good conversation for the next four wartime years. "You must forgive if I send in return a scrawl traced by a hand shaking with fatigue, & guided by a brain wobbling with imbecility," she wrote to Bernard Berenson. "I'm not used to philanthropy, & since I got back & took over my work-room . . . I've been at it every day from 8 a.m. till dinner. As soon as peace is declared I shall renounce good works forever!"

Most of the Americans in Paris had no intention of living in the middle of a country at war. They'd come to Paris for culture and color and fun. Now they wanted out. Edith had no patience with these people. She was glad when they finally boarded trains and boats and left.

Others stayed in France but continued to carry on as if nothing out of the ordinary were happening. Edith had no patience with them, either. She even became irked with Walter Berry. "Walter tries to pretend, by means of . . . a restaurant table, and a new cigarette case, that he is still Seeing Life in the good old Ritzian style," she wrote Bernard Berenson.

And some rose gallantly to the occasion. Among them was young Percy Lubbock, who was staying in Edith's guest suite and doing research in various hospitals for the Red Cross.

A second "army" descended on Paris—an army of refugees. Among them were the Belgians and French whose villages had been destroyed by the German army on its march toward Paris. Before the war, the refugees' knowledge of world events was "measured by the shadow of their village steeple." Now, Edith wrote in an article for *Scribner's Magazine*, they were in Paris, "people who stand in hundreds every day outside the doors of the shelters improvised to rescue them, and who receive, in return for the loss of everything that makes life sweet . . . a cot in a dormitory, a meal-ticket—and perhaps, on lucky days, a pair of shoes."

Refugees by the thousands were overwhelming the Franco-Belgian organization that was trying to take care of them. Would Mrs. Wharton form a committee to help with the refugees? And money was sorely needed. Would she raise some? Edith had her hands full overseeing her workroom. But yes, Mrs. Wharton would see what she could do. Edith contacted Minnie Jones to see if her sister-in-law could organize fundraising efforts in America, begging from the very society people she'd satirized in her stories. Edith Wharton committees sprang up in New York, Boston, Washington, Philadelphia, and Providence. Edith remembered these distant "friends and strangers" working with her "as untiringly as those who were close at hand." Over the next year, Edith, through her committees, would raise $82,000, the equivalent of well over a million dollars today. With these funds, she and a group of friends in France formed a second charity: the American Hostels for Refugees. Edith was determined that her new charity would provide not only food and housing but medical services, employment, and education for children. By the end of 1915, the first full year of the war, nine thousand refugees had received assistance.

If Edith's donors were going to keep giving, they had to know how urgent the need was. Edith began a new kind of writing: reports to contributors. It wasn't as satisfying as writing fiction, but these reports and her articles for *Scribner's Magazine* took up the bulk of her writing time. When she wasn't writing or fundraising, she worked. According to Percy Lubbock, Edith "could stimulate, she could fire by her example, she could see that nothing went flat or stale in the doing." But she desperately needed more help—organizational help for the long haul—and volunteers were usually flighty and undependable. One day a woman Edith had met socially a few years earlier, Elisina Tyler, knocked on her door and said simply, "My husband and I want to help you. How can you use us?"

No one would have banked on a successful partnership between these two women. They were both strong willed and independent. Both were, as their kindest critics said, "difficult." Thirty-nine-year-old Elisina Tyler was strikingly beautiful, but Bernard Berenson found her so overbearing that he could hardly stand her. Many of Edith's friends shared Berenson's opinion. Besides, Elisina and her husband had a four-year-old son, and Edith's world had never included children.

Edith, however, recognized Elisina Tyler's true worth. Elisina was fluent in French, Italian, and English, and she was strong enough to take charge and make things happen. The two clicked almost immediately. As Edith remembered it, Elisina found the American Hostels for Refugees "a tottering house of cards, and turned it into solid bricks and mortar. Never once did she fail me for an hour, never did we disagree, never did her energy flag."

• • •

A day nursery for children suffering from tuberculosis of the bone was part of Edith's second war charity, the American Hostels for Refugees.

• • •

Elisina Tyler. When she volunteered to help Edith with her charity work, she referred to herself as "Mrs. Tyler" even though she had left her first husband and three older children in England and was not yet married to Royall Tyler. Minnie and Beatrix Jones found this shocking, but Edith and Elisina became devoted lifelong friends.

And little Bill Tyler somehow found his way straight into Edith's heart. He called her Edoo, and she began inviting him over for lunch. Edith told him he was welcome to bring his mother, but only if she behaved.

In April 1915, the Belgian government turned to Edith for help. She'd done so much . . . but could she possibly organize some relief for orphaned children and the elderly? Mrs. Wharton could. Edith and Elisina founded a third charity, the Children of Flanders Rescue Committee. A group of Belgian girls arrived in Paris at four in the morning, looking like "little widows," according to Elisina, in their black clothes.

Next, a hundred nuns arrived, then a colony of elderly women, then six hundred children who had been found scavenging for food in the trenches. Could Mrs. Wharton . . . ? Mrs. Wharton could. "All the Belgians in Paris are feeding out of Edith's hands," Walter Berry told Bernard Berenson. "She's half a wreck but keeps on." Only an end to the war would lighten her load.

Edith was sure that if the United States would come to France's aid, the tide would turn. She wrote to Minnie Jones that she was "not very proud just now of being an American." France had been attacked for no reason, and she didn't see why the United States was still sitting on the sidelines. If America only knew how awful the trenches were and how many were dying. With the unflappable Cook driving, Edith and Walter began making trips to the frontline to deliver clothes and medicines and, more important, to gather information for articles that might convince the United States to come to France's defense.

On a trip to Verdun, Edith and Walter stumbled upon a church late one afternoon and Edith captured the scene in an article for *Scribner's Magazine*. Entering the nave, they saw "four rows of wooden cots with brown blankets. In almost every one lay a soldier . . . few of them wounded, the greater number stricken with fever, bronchitis, frost-bite, pleurisy, or some other form of trench-sickness." As Edith and Walter looked on, a bell rang, and soldiers and villagers arrived for a vesper service. Latin chants were followed by a canticle that had been composed during the war of 1870. "The women wailed it near the altar, the soldiers took it up from the door in stronger tones; but the bodies in the cots never stirred, and more and more, as the day faded, the church looked like a quiet grave-yard in a battle-field."

In her passion over the unjust battering France was enduring, Edith easily wrote many such articles. What she couldn't do, during that first year of the war, was write fiction. She'd had high hopes for *Literature*, the novel she'd started just before her world crashed. But she wrote to

• • •

Edith's Children of Flanders Rescue Committee charity, her third, served not only children but the elderly.
These three women were cared for at a facility in Sevres, France.

Bernard Berenson that "things have killed it—one thing after another."

She turned her writing attention to a "literary salad I am mixing in a last passionate effort to raise money." The "salad" was a collection of essays and poems and artwork contributed by friends and friends-of-friends. It was called *The Book of the Homeless*, and she hoped the proceeds would help fund her charities. Her old friend Paul Bourget contributed an essay in which he wrote: "What was the war of 1870 to this one? This time there will be a different ending. . . . There must be."

And of course Henry James wrote a piece for the book. Henry, who had once been appalled by Edith's fearsome energy, was now all admiration and support as he watched her from the other side of the English Channel. Now in his seventies, he wrote to her that he was "condemned . . . by doddering age & 'mean' infirmity," so he couldn't make the same kind of contribution to the war effort that Edith was making. But he could applaud her tireless work: "You're magnificent & I am thrilled, & can't sufficiently rejoice in you and be proud of you." In his essay for *The Book of the Homeless*, the great Henry James—"the Master," as he was known—expressed how humble he felt next to the man (or woman) of deeds. "I *am* so struck with the charm, as I can only call it, of the tone and temper of the man of action," he wrote. His words seemed useless to him in the face of this war. He was envious of those—like Edith and the soldiers at the front—who could *do*.

The essay Henry James contributed to *The Book of the Homeless* may well have been his last piece of writing. In December 1915, his secretary wrote to Edith that her old friend had suffered a stroke and was near death. "There is nothing to do now," Edith wrote Minnie Jones, "but to wish that 'all that mighty heart were lying still.'" Henry James's death came two months later, on February 28, 1916. "He died without suffering, while asleep," Edith wrote to a mutual friend. "I am happy to think that the end came so peacefully, and sooner than one could hope; but my life is so diminished by this death."

She turned her attention back to the war. It needed to be won, for Henry's sake, but she was growing weary of the charitable tasks she'd taken up on the home front. They were not only strenuous, they were a poor fit for her. "Everything I did during the war in the way of charitable work was forced on me by the necessities of the hour, but always with the sense that others would have done it far better," she observed in her autobiography. To Bernard Berenson she wrote, "The worst of doing good is that it makes one forget how to do anything more interesting."

But France was deeply grateful for the good works that had been forced on Edith Wharton. In March 1916 she was made a Chevalier of the Legion of Honor, France's highest and most distinguished award. Edith was mightily pleased, especially since the government had decided not to give this award to civilians or foreigners for the duration of the war and had made an exception in her case. Eighty-seven letters of congratulation poured in on a single day. A French newspaper wrote that Edith's "enormous and varied work is a silent work . . . hidden beneath an air, hard to describe, of deceptive nonchalance, of smiling grace—an air of having really nothing to do in life and no other concern." The most touching response came from the women of Edith's workroom. It was a scroll designed by the seamstresses expressing their deepest thanks "for your attachment to this *Ouvroir* [workplace] which you love so much and which has kept us alive now for twenty months." Fifty-seven workwomen signed it.

Spring 1916 brought another ray of sunshine. Edith was able to write a book, her first since *The Custom of the Country* was published, just before the war. She had abandoned the novel *Literature* and started something completely new. It was called *Summer,* and like *Ethan Frome,* it was set in a small, ordinary town in the mountains of western Massachusetts. "I do not remember ever visualizing with more intensity the inner scene [of any other novel], or the creatures peopling it," she later wrote. It was a bleak, almost scandalous novel in which the orphaned heroine, Charity Royall, becomes pregnant by a young man who abandons her for a more proper woman. Charity is left with no choice but to marry her elderly guardian. It wasn't the plot, but the pure joy of writing a story after so long, that lifted Edith's spirits.

Unfortunately, when Edith left the fictional world of *Summer* and returned to the real world, the war was still there. Soldiers were not only dying by bullets and bombs; tuberculosis was raging through the dirt and the damp of the trenches. So while Edith continued to complain of

• • •

Edith and Walter Berry (right) with two officers on one of the five trips they took to the battlefront in 1915.

fatigue and long hours, she opened a fourth charity, a group of convalescent homes for victims of tuberculosis. She insisted she was at the end of her energy, that she got no joy from her philanthropy. And yet she couldn't see a need without rising to meet it.

On November 11, 1916, Bill Tyler celebrated his sixth birthday. Edith couldn't attend his party but sent him a gift and a note. She closed with the words "I want very much to see you again, and hope you will soon come to lunch with me."

James Montgomery Flagg created this recruiting poster in 1917, after the United States entered the Great War on the side of the Allies.

Paris that winter of 1917 was bitterly cold. "For the last ten days we've been having the kind of weather I left New York to escape from," Edith wrote to Bernard Berenson, "blinding sky, grinding cold, searching dust." She celebrated her own birthday—her fifty-fifth—with pipes frozen and light provided by candles. By the end of February it was no better. "The cold is still grim," she wrote. And the war continued.

Edith came down with a bad case of the flu, and the indomitable Elisina was on the verge of a breakdown. She had learned that a son from her first marriage had died and had tried to overcome her grief through work. In America, sixty-seven-year-old Minnie Jones was on a third fundraising tour, managing accounts, proofreading organizational reports, and translating war articles. How long could they go on? It seemed that the civilian "war" in Paris was going as badly as the one being fought on the frontlines.

In April 1917 came news that renewed everyone's energy. The United States finally declared war on Germany. Now Edith could hold her head up again. Now there was hope that the tide would turn. On the same day that he brought the United States into the war, President Wilson issued a statement asking for people to channel all donations to charities, such as Edith's, to the American Red Cross instead. This too was welcome news. It looked as if the Red Cross would assume the management of her charities, so Edith could step aside and get back to her former life.

The Germans began shelling Paris with new long-range guns, including one the Allies called Big Bertha, after its inventor's wife. Edith wrote to a friend: "The chief interest of this letter will be due to the fact of its being written during an air raid—the first daylight one that Paris has been favored with since the famous attack in the beginning of the war. . . . It is now 9:45, & since 8 o'c there has been a good deal of booming . . . & sirening in Paris."

The first four of the German offensives of 1918 succeeded in pushing the battle line deep into French territory. In Percy Lubbock's words, "The immovable war that had shaped our lives for so long, suddenly heaved and lurched, the huge line swayed and sagged against us—not away from us, but nearer and nearer." By May 27, 1918, the road to Paris was unprotected. Not since the first Battle of the Marne River, which Edith had "watched" from England back in 1914, had Paris been in such danger.

The Allied line sagged, but it never broke. The Americans seemed inefficient to the veteran French and British, but they were eager and determined and enthusiastic. They brought heart to a war that was grim with disillusionment.

Edith also showed she had heart. She began negotiating to buy a house in one of the northern suburbs of Paris that had

• • •

An Allied soldier photographed Edith seeing an ambulance convoy off to the front in 1916.

been abandoned when the Germans began their advance. With the purchase of that house, Edith demonstrated her conviction that Paris would withstand this attack, that Paris would not become a German city, that the Allies would prevail.

The crucial point in 1918—the beginning of the fifth and last year of the war—came on July 15, when the Germans succeeded in crossing the Marne River, and it looked as if the fifth of their offensives would succeed. But the French were determined that these most unwelcome guests would have a short stay. In just three days, the Germans were pushed back across the Marne.

Two months later, Erich Ludendorff, the German general who had masterminded the offensives of 1918, shut himself in his office and flew into a blind rage. His strategy had failed, and Germany's army, people, and politicians were tired. They wanted peace. Germany had to ask France for an armistice.

TEN

I Want to Go Home

You ought to buy it. . . . It's just the place for a
solitary-minded devil like you.
"Kerfol," short story, 1916

The news that the war had finally ended came to Paris on a "hushed November day." It was bells, not words, that made the announcement. "The quarter I lived in was so quiet in those days," Edith remembered, "that, except for the crash of aerial battles, few sounds disturbed it." But on that particular day in 1918, she heard the bells of a nearby church ringing at an unusual hour. She and her household servants rushed out to the balcony. From there they heard, "one after another, the bells of Paris calling to each other . . . and we knew the war was over."

Paris paused and took a look at itself. There was a gaping crater in the Tuileries rose garden where a bomb had fallen. The chestnut trees

that had once lined the grand boulevards had been cut down for fire-
wood during the long, cold winters. The stained glass windows of Notre
Dame had been removed for safekeeping and replaced with dull yellow
panes. Piles of rubble were everywhere. Men with arms and legs miss-
ing begged on street corners. Nearly half the women of the city were in
mourning.

It was to Paris—Edith's beautiful, sad, enraged, violated city—that
people from around the world came to take part in the peace talks
that followed what was now being called the Great War. Many of the
Americans who arrived took up residence in Edith's favorite hotel, the
Crillon, where they were dazzled by the old-world luxury. Old-
fashioned charm had its limits, however. The hydraulic elevators in the
hotel were laughable. Who in America would put up with elevators that
had to stop between floors while water moved from tank to tank? "Before we get through with these fellows over here we will teach them how
to do things and how to do them quickly," a young American boasted. It
was just the kind of comment that made Edith cringe.

These international visitors brought with them the giddy, hopeful
sense that, after four years and three months of destruction, war would
become a thing of the past. The Paris peace talks would create a bright
new world. Who would want to be anywhere else?

Edith Wharton, for one. She wrote to Berenson that the city had become dreadfully crowded and busy and noisy. Edith, along with her
maid and Robert Norton, fled to a hotel in the village of Hyères on the
south coast of France.

Bernard Berenson was dismayed at Edith's departure and told her
so in a letter. How could she leave Paris at such an exciting moment?
"It has taken days & days of healing silence, & warm sun & long walks,
to get the poison out of my bones," she wrote him from Hyères. "But
now I'm getting as lively as a cricket." She was more than ready to hand
over politics and the creation of a new world order to diplomats and

heads of state. Edith Wharton would create her own new world. She would return to her writing and her gardening. She would gather her circle of friends close around her again, and they would talk and laugh and eat together as they had before the war.

Once it was restored to its former glory, and to Edith's exacting standards, the property just outside Paris that she had bought near the end of the war would serve as a gathering place. When she purchased it, it was called Villa Jean-Marie, but Edith discovered that in the mid-1700s the house had been named after two sisters—actresses whose stage name was Colombe and who were housed there by their lovers. The story intrigued Edith, and she decided to restore its original name: Pavillon Colombe ("dove pavilion"). She would spend summer and fall there each year. Pavillon Colombe was close enough to Paris for her to enjoy the city she loved, and it was large enough for her to plant a garden.

Edith thought that a second home on the southern coast of France, where she could spend her winters away from Pavillon Colombe and the cold of Paris and have a garden all year round, would also be wonderful. Wandering around Hyères with Robert Norton, she stumbled on a crumbling old chateau. Paul and Minnie Bourget came south to have a look at it and couldn't believe Edith was thinking of buying such a sad heap of a place for a winter home. The work on Pavillon Colombe wasn't even finished.

What the Bourgets saw as a pile of rubble looked like the perfect winter retreat to Edith. It had been built within the walls of a monastery called St. Claire, so that's what Edith called it. She threw herself into the restoration of not one but two neglected old mansions. In August 1919 she moved into Pavillon Colombe, outside Paris. A year and a half later she spent her first winter at St. Claire. "We moved in *at last* two days before Xmas," she wrote to Minnie Jones. By "we," she meant herself, Robert Norton, Gaillard Lapsley, and the "faithful household." It was the happiest Christmas she had spent in a long time and the first gathering of what came to be known as the St. Claire Christmas Club. A winter picnic became an established part of their celebration.

For the remaining years of her life, Edith would spend summer and fall at Pavillon Colombe, near Paris, and winter and spring at St. Claire in Hyères. Walter Berry agreed to take over the lease to her apartment in Paris, number 53 rue de Varenne, which had been her home for nine years.

The Great War seemed to have cracked history into two pieces. That faraway time called "before the war" felt unreal, like a fairy tale, and there was no going back to it. French salons like Rosa's that had flourished before 1914 were no more. The war had destroyed old buildings and churches, and, with them, a certain hope and innocence. It was hard to begin to dream again after such bloody years.

The war had also changed the reading public. Edith the writer couldn't shut herself into her two mansions and ignore this fact if she was going to continue to publish. Her initial instinct was to write about the war itself. But her first war novella, *The Marne*, was considered old-fashioned and overly patriotic. Her second, *A Son at the Front*, had trouble finding a publisher. No one wanted to read about the war anymore. When the novel finally came out in 1923, the reviews were terrible. Critics found the book outdated, disagreeable, and disappointing. One called it "a belated essay in propaganda."

So Edith couldn't write about the war. And she couldn't make sense of the postwar world that felt as if it were shifting right under her feet. What was Edith Wharton the writer to do? For her next novel, she decided to reach back in time to the Old New York of her childhood, the world of Caroline Astor and Ward McAllister that was stifling, but also comfortingly stable. The book would be called *The Age of Innocence.* Perhaps if she could grab hold of something familiar, she could steady herself before attempting a novel set in this bewildering postwar civilization.

• • •

Elisina Tyler discovered the house that would become Pavillon Colombe and pointed it out to Edith.

The Age of Innocence seemed to pour out of Edith. She completed it in just over seven months. It was much more than a simple story about the rigid manners of an earlier time. It had something to say about the postwar world in which her readers lived. In *The Age of Innocence*, one critic observed, Edith Wharton "laughs at the . . . tyranny of . . . rigid social taboos." But at the same time, "she has painted them at full length, to hang upon our walls, where they . . . utter a silent reproof to our scrambling vulgarities."

Edith well knew how crippling society's rules could be. But when those rules were swept away, "old landmarks . . . sign-posts and the danger signals" were swept away too. She had been hemmed in by society's expectations. But there was something about the order and regularity of Old New York that Edith loved and missed, now that it was gone.

"You bring back that time as if it were last week," Minnie Jones marveled after reading the first few chapters. Walter was also impressed. But he didn't think the book would sell. "We are the last people left who can remember New York and Newport as they were then," he told Edith, "and nobody else will be interested." Edith knew it was a good book, but secretly she agreed with Walter. If people didn't want to read about the war, why in the world would they buy a book about events even further back in time? Walter was right, she decided. No one would read it.

As it turned out, both Edith and Walter were completely wrong. *The Age of Innocence*, published in 1920, was an instant hit. Readers devoured it; critics praised it. "It is one of the best novels of the twentieth century," the *New York Times* proclaimed, "and looks like a permanent addition to literature." *The Age of Innocence* was awarded the prestigious Pulitzer Prize for fiction, making Edith the first woman to achieve such an honor.

• • •

Taken in the early 1920s, this publicity photo shows Edith dressed in deliberately old-fashioned style. It was used as the frontispiece for her 1934 autobiography, A Backward Glance.

The wild success of *The Age of Innocence* should have given Edith the confidence to move forward with her next novel. But when she looked around at the literary scene, what Edith saw was a herd of so-called new writers. It wasn't just their subject matter that was different; they were using an entirely new style of writing called stream of consciousness. Just follow a character's thoughts and there's your book. Edith didn't much like either the new writing style or the new writers. They were just too lazy to think up plots for their books. Take James Joyce, whose novel *Ulysses* had every-

· · ·

Edith's friend Robert Norton, who was with her when she first stumbled on St. Claire, painted this watercolor of Edith's winter home after it was renovated.

one absolutely raving. Edith thought the book was "a turgid welter of pornography (the rudest schoolboy kind) & unformed & unimportant drivel, & until the raw ingredients of a pudding *make* a pudding," she explained to Bernard Berenson, "I shall never believe that the raw material of sensation & thought can make a work of art without the cook's intervening."

If it had been only James Joyce, Edith could have ignored the whole thing. But Virginia Woolf and T. S. Eliot and others were also getting raves for their formless stuff. Edith wrote a series of articles for *Scribner's Magazine* on how to go about writing a proper story. These articles were gathered into a book called *The Writing of Fiction*, which came out in 1925.

Even as she criticized them, Edith began to suspect that she was some kind of relic and that these "new writers" were leaving her behind. Just before *The Writing of Fiction* came out, she wrote to an old friend: "I am really turning into a green shade as I sit undisturbed under my elms . . . but as my work reaches its close, I feel so sure that it is either nothing, or far more than they know. . . . And I wonder, a little

Edith wore jewelry with her academic robe when she received her honorary degree from Yale in 1923.

desolately, which?" She was afraid she had become "a deplorable example of what people used to read in the Dark Ages."

Some young writers clearly respected her work. One of them, Sinclair Lewis, sent her a letter of congratulation when *The Age of Innocence* won the Pulitzer Prize. That letter meant a lot to Edith.

And when she made her very last trip back to the United States in 1923, she found that another young writer, F. Scott Fitzgerald, idolized her to distraction. She made the journey to accept an honorary doctorate from Yale University and took the opportunity to visit New York and meet with Charles Scribner, who was publishing some of her books again. Stories began to circulate about that meeting. It was said that Fitzgerald burst in unannounced. According to one version, he threw himself at Edith's feet; according to another, he tried to throw himself out the window.

Fitzgerald saw himself as Edith's literary descendant because he too wrote about high society. Two years after their New York encounter, Fitzgerald sent Edith a copy of his book *The Great Gatsby*. Edith wrote him a note saying she was "touched" that he would even acknowledge an older writer who must seem to him "the literary equivalent of tufted furniture and gas chandeliers." She invited him to visit her at Pavillon Colombe. That meeting was as big a disaster as the one in New York. Fitzgerald was so nervous at the thought of being in the presence of the great Edith Wharton that he arrived drunk. Conversation stalled, and in trying to revive it, Fitzgerald got tangled up in a very pointless, very crude story. After he left, Edith wrote in her diary "To tea . . . Scott Fitzgerald, the novelist (horrible)."

Whatever her literary reputation in the postwar world, Edith was making money from her writing. Lots of money. And she intended to use it. In 1926, at the age of sixty-four, she paid half the expenses to charter a yacht with four friends and cruise the Aegean for ten weeks.

Later that same year, she took a run through northern Italy. Her only companion on this trip was Walter Berry. She still treasured his company above anyone else's. Before they set out, Walter had written her a letter reminding her of that summer, years ago, when they'd first met at Bar Harbor and he'd left without proposing. In his letter, he reminded her of their romantic afternoon canoeing on the lake and told her how he lay awake that night "wondering and wondering." He reminded her of the time, fourteen years later, when he and Edith met again at Land's End and he found himself wondering why he *"hadn't—* for it would have been *good. "* His letter closed with words that reassured Edith that all the young, beautiful women with whom he always seemed to be flirting didn't hold a candle to her. "I've never 'wondered' about anyone else," he wrote, "and there wouldn't be much of me if you were cut out of it. Forty years of it is you, dear."

That trip to Italy would be their last. On October 2, 1927, just over a year after their return, Walter suffered a stroke. Too proud to allow anyone to see him reduced to a "stuttering paralytic," he locked himself away with his servants and his doctors in his apartment at number 53 rue de Varenne. He was almost completely paralyzed and unable to speak, but he made it clear to Jules, his valet, that he didn't want to see anyone.

Edith waited for seven days, unwilling to violate his wish to be alone. She understood Walter's fierce pride. But she also knew the depth of their feelings for each other. She was glad they'd never married. There was what Elisina called a "dreadful devouring quality" in romantic love that might have destroyed their precious friendship. Edith was closer to Walter Berry than to any of the other men in her life, including Morton

• • •

Advertising The Age of Innocence, *the publisher called Edith "America's Greatest Woman Novelist."*

Fullerton. Edith's great fear was that Walter's pride would force him to die without their meeting one last time.

On October 9, Jules sent word that Walter wanted to see her. She came immediately. For the next three days she sat by him for a short time each morning and each afternoon. She held him and spoke to him of old friends and old times. When she visited on October 11, he held her and kissed her and called her "dear." On October 12, 1927, Edith wrote in her diary, "The Love of all my life died today, & I with him."

When Walter passed away, Edith was sixty-five and no stranger to loss. Henry James, Anna Bahlmann, Egerton Winthrop, and Edith's brother Freddy had all died during the war. Howard Sturgis, Sally Norton, Rosa de Fitz-James, and her best-loved brother Harry had passed away in the years following it. But none of these losses compared to Walter's.

Elisina rushed to Paris to be with Edith when she learned of Walter's death. Other friends and the household servants watched anxiously, wondering if this might break her. Several weeks after his death, Edith went with Walter's sister to number 53 rue de Varenne, found the letters she had written to him over the years of their friendship, and burned them, one by one, in the fireplace.

To Bernard Berenson she wrote: "I feel totally rudderless." And to John Hugh-Smith: "I perceive now that I, who thought I loved solitude, was never for one moment alone—& a great desert lies ahead of me. . . . I sometimes feel I am too old to live through such hours, & take up the daily round again."

But she did indeed "take up the daily round." To Mary Berenson she wrote: "At my age, and with a will-to-live (and to work) as strong as mine one comes soon, I find, to accept sorrows and renunciations, and to *build* with them, instead of letting them tear me down. . . . So I go on—" She recorded her grief and pain in her journal. But when she left Paris for St. Claire two months after Walter's death, she'd finished her

. . .

Daisy Chanler (left) accompanied Edith (right) on her second
Mediterranean cruise aboard the Osprey.

next novel, *The Children*. It was the first book she had ever written that Walter didn't read before publication.

Another death followed hard on the heels of Walter's. In February 1928 she received a cable telling her that Teddy Wharton had died in New York. The two men who had entered her life one after the other that long-ago summer at Bar Harbor had also left it in close succession.

Though Edith had not communicated with Teddy for years, she'd followed his slow, agonizing slide into insanity through news from friends. Since Nannie's death in 1921, he had been in the care of a devoted nurse. The man who had been "sunshine in the house," the all-American outdoorsman, the kind host who loved wine and food and socializing, spent each day of his last years sitting in a chair with a shawl around his shoulders, completely alone.

Edith's mind reached back to the good years they'd had. To a mutual friend she wrote: "You will go back to the far-off past of our youths together, as I do tonight, and will remember many things that I am remembering. . . . Teddy was the kindest of companions till that dreadful blighting illness came upon him, and you knew how much I appreciated his good qualities, and for how many years I struggled to carry on some sort of life with him."

Under the influence of Egerton Winthrop and Walter Berry, Edith had converted from the Episcopalian doctrine of her childhood to what was known as scientific rationalism: Reason, not faith, became her guide. But these early mentors were now gone, and in the last decade of her life, Edith became fascinated by questions scientific rationalism couldn't answer. In 1931 and again in 1932, she visited Rome and

• • •

Walter Berry and Edith on one of their many picnics.

attended church services with a young Catholic woman, Nicky Mariano, who was a member of Bernard Berenson's staff. Nicky was afraid her famous companion would be bored by something as unintellectual as a religious service. Instead, Nicky observed, the mass seemed to carry Edith away "into another sphere."

The characters in Edith's later novels reflected on spiritual things. In *Twilight Sleep*, published in 1927, several characters search comically, but also a bit pathetically, for the next new spiritual guru. They skip from the "Mahatma" (who required too much time to fix what ailed them) to the great teacher Alvah Loft, described as author of a book called *Spiritual Vacuum-Cleaning*.

When readers meet Vance Weston, the hero of another novel called

• • •

Edith at her desk at Pavillon Colombe, 1931.

Hudson River Bracketed, he has just graduated from college and invented a new religion. By the end of the book, Vance Weston has concluded that "the greatest proof of the validity of a religion was its age, its duration, its having stood through centuries of change." Nicky and others wondered if Edith had secretly converted to Catholicism.

Edith herself thought a lot about how to approach the business of getting old. Some of her characters battled against it with beauty treatments and various cures, and they were always pitifully unsuccessful. Not Edith. Instead of shrinking from old age, she saw how wonderful the later years of life could be. When Minnie Jones wrote sadly from New York about the "woes and privations of old age," Edith responded: "The farther I have penetrated into this ill-famed Valley the more full of interest, and beauty too, have I found it. It is full of its own quiet radiance, and in that light I discover many enchanting details which the midday dazzle obscured."

As her health began to fail, her will to enjoy every last minute of life grew. In March 1929 she nearly died of pneumonia, and Elisina was called in to nurse her back to health. It turned out Edith Wharton wasn't ready for her own story to end just yet, and she rallied. There was more traveling to be done: a trip to England, to Rome, to Wales (she had always wanted to see Wales!). And there were more stories to tell. Her novel *Hudson River Bracketed* came out on schedule in November 1929, and a short story collection, *Certain People*, six months later. In 1932 came a novel called *The Gods Arrive*, the sequel to *Hudson River Bracketed*.

That same year, she began writing her autobiography, *A Backward Glance*. For a woman who had spent her life exposing the truth in her novels, it is surprising that her autobiography left significant truths about her own life untold. In it she says nothing about her failed marriage, or her divorce, or the broken relationships with her mother and brothers. Morton Fullerton is never mentioned.

In April 1935, at age seventy-three, she came down with the flu and then various heart problems, and for a second time Elisina was called. But Edith was needed in England, where Minnie Jones had died unexpectedly. So she rallied again and crossed the channel to see to her sister-in-law's funeral. By spring 1936 she was entertaining again at St. Claire, and a new short story collection, *The World Over*, was published. Some thought it the best she'd ever written. In October she wrote to Mary Berenson of "this wonderful adventure of living, which seems to me to pile up its glories like an horizon-wide sunset as the light declines. I'm afraid I'm an incorrigible life-lover & life-wonderer & adventurer."

The last gathering of the St. Claire Christmas Club took place in December 1936. The hostess and the guests at that final gathering loved and irritated one another in the way only old friends can. John Hugh-Smith, the youngest member of Edith's inner circle, was fifty-five and a bit deaf. He had taken to shouting. Gaillard Lapsley, whose friendship with Edith had started in America and blossomed when he moved to England, had grown somewhat pompous and self-righteous. Edith constantly interrupted the conversation to fuss and fidget with the table and the food and her dogs until Robert Norton, the one who'd been with her when she'd first stumbled on St. Claire just after the war, told her to sit down.

The annual picnic had become something of a chore. No one had the courage to tell Edith she was the only one who enjoyed it anymore. But not one of those gathered at St. Claire that Christmas would have traded the occasion for the world.

In the first few months of 1937, Edith visited a seamstress to be fitted for some new clothes. She motored around Hyères with Robert Norton and worked on a new novel, *The Buccaneers*, which she would never complete. She submitted a short story called "All Souls" to her agent. She called herself an invalid but claimed she didn't mind it at all. She wrote Bernard Berenson that this stage of life was "full of oases &

• • •

The last meeting of the St. Claire Christmas Club, 1936. Seated (left to right) are John Hugh-Smith, a friend named Madame Homberg, and Edith; standing are (left) Robert Norton and Gaillard Lapsley.

hidden springs." Berenson found this slowed-down version of his old friend better than ever: "She no longer outstrides and out-lives me," he observed.

On April 16, Linky, the Pekingese dog who had been with Edith for eleven years, died. In a letter to Elisina's son, Bill, now grown and

Feb 25'23

KNICKERBOCKER CLUB

Dearest — The real dream — mine — was in the canoe and in the night, afterwards, — for I lay awake wondering and wondering, — and then, when morning came, wondering how I could have wondered, — I, a $less lawyer (not even that, yet) with just about enough cash for the canoe and for Rodick's bill —

And then, later, in the little cottage at Newport, I wondered why I hadn't, — for it would all have been good, — and then the slices of years slid by.

Well, my dear, I've never "wondered" about any one else, and there wouldn't be much of me if you were cut out of it. Forty years of it in you, dear — W.

• • •

Dated February 25, 1923, this is one of the few letters from
Walter Berry that Edith didn't burn after his death.

married, she wrote, "We really communicated with each other—and no one had such wise things to say as Linky."

Edith began the yearly motor trip from St. Claire to Pavillon Colombe in May. She stopped to visit her on-again-off-again friend Ogden Codman, who was living south of Paris. At his home she had a heart attack but was alert enough to scold Codman: "This will teach you not to ask decrepit old ladies to stay." She finished the trip to Pavillon Colombe by ambulance. For the third and last time, Edith called for Elisina Tyler, and she came immediately. Sensing that the end was near, Elisina kept a journal of her last ten weeks with Edith. "We lived through one of the loveliest summers I have known, side by side, with content and with fear," Elisina wrote.

Bill Tyler and his wife, Betsy, arrived, and Edith was overjoyed to see them. The couple wheeled her through the garden so she could feed the fish in her pond. Betsy asked how old goldfish could grow to be. "Oh, up to about 75," Edith told her. "As old as *that*?" Bill exclaimed. "Well, it isn't so bad when you get there," Edith told him with a smile.

Beatrix Jones Farrand, Freddy's disinherited daughter and the last remaining descendant of Frederic and Lucretia Jones, came to visit. A steady, quiet stream of old friends also stopped in. Once, when it was too rainy to be out in the garden, Edith pulled out the scrapbook Anna Bahlmann had made for her and leafed through the pages of her own remarkable writing life.

In their last days together, Edith talked to Elisina about her relationship with Walter Berry. She said he had once written her a real love letter. She also spoke of Teddy. "He enjoyed life so much. . . . There was no cruelty and no unkindness in him. Yet he was cruel and unkind through weakness." In her journal, Elisina noted one of Edith's favorite comments: "Impulses and emotions have their value; but the sovereign mind must rule."

By the evening of August 7, Edith's words had become confused, her thoughts disconnected. "I want to go home," she said. "Where is Madame Tyler?" Knowing that Edith's "sovereign mind . . . had abdicated its rule," Elisina replied, "It's all right dearest. I am here with you." Edith Wharton slipped from consciousness. She died four days later, on August 11, 1937.

Edith had been very specific about her funeral. There would be no long procession through the streets of Paris. Her friends would please meet at the church, and she would be brought along in a simple hearse. An honor guard consisting of local firemen and war veterans gathered in the courtyard of Pavillon Colombe and stood at attention as her oaken coffin was carried out. She was buried in a grave near Walter Berry's at the Cimetière des Gonards at Versailles. The inscription on her coffin read: *O Crux Ave Spes Unica*—"Hail O Cross, our only hope." She had settled the debate between faith and reason.

Out of the "family" of servants who had been with Edith over the years, only Alfred White was still with her. Catherine Gross had died in 1933 and was buried in Hyères. Cook had suffered a heart attack in 1923, which kept him from doing any more driving. Edith had provided him and his wife with a generous pension so they could return to America to live. White, hired in 1888, when Edith and Teddy were just back from their Mediterranean cruise, was left to do the mourning on behalf of Edith's faithful staff. "Now it's all over," White wrote to Bernard Berenson. "I can't believe she's gone forever—it seems she's on one of her little motor trips and will come back again."

The Gist of Me

What's the use of making mysteries?
It only makes people want to nose 'em out.

The Age of Innocence, *1920*

"For My Biographer," Edith wrote on a packet of papers before she died. She wanted the person who ended up telling the story of her life to "find the gist of me." But she so completely erased all traces of Morton Fullerton that when scholars read her Love Diary, they assumed that the unnamed "you" to whom she wrote was Walter Berry. For thirty years following her death, the "gist" of Edith Wharton was an intelligent, grandly proper woman whose male acquaintances (including her husband) were never more than close friends.

In 1967, the discovery of a letter from Morton Fullerton to Elisina Tyler brought the brief affair to light and sent scholars scrambling to reassess her image. Thirty years after her death, Edith Wharton became human. Perhaps that was exactly what she intended. Perhaps the fact that she didn't destroy her Love Diary suggests that she wanted the real story told, after scholars had taken some years to puzzle it out and all the major players in the drama were safely dead and gone.

In her lifetime, Edith Wharton managed to live properly in society while escaping from the restrictions that might have kept her from writing. Thirty years after her death, she made another escape: from her stiff, passionless society image to "the gist of me." And because the years had softened scandal into history, she had, once again, made her escape properly.

•   •   •

Milou, Mija, and Nicette.

· ABBREVIATIONS USED IN THE NOTES ·

A	*The Age of Innocence,* EW
AG	Alice Warder Garrett
Astor	Homberger, *Mrs. Astor's New York*
BB	Bernard Berenson
Beinecke	Edith Wharton Collection, Yale University
BG	*A Backward Glance,* EW
BH	*The Book of the Homeless,* EW
Bio, Lee	Lee, *Edith Wharton*
Bio, Lewis	Lewis, *Edith Wharton: A Biography*
BJF	Beatrix Jones Farrand
CS	Charles Scribner
CV	*The Cruise of the Vanadis,* EW
Dwight	Dwight, *Edith Wharton: An Extraordinary Life*
EF	*Ethan Frome,* EW
ELB	Edward L. Burlingame
End	Price, *The End of the Age of Innocence*
ET	Elisina Tyler
EW	Edith Wharton
EWHJ	Bell, *Edith Wharton & Henry James*

EWN	*Edith Wharton: Novellas and Other Writings,* EW
EWW	Emelyn Washburn
FF	*Fighting France,* EW
Firestone	Firestone Library, Princeton
First 400	Patterson, *The First Four Hundred*
FL	*Fast and Loose & The Buccaneers,* EW
FPK	Dr. Francis P. Kinnicutt
FT	*The Fruit of the Tree,* EW
FW	*French Ways and Their Meaning,* EW
Garrett	Alice Warder Garrett Archives
GL	Gaillard Lapsley
GS	Geoffrey Scott
HJ	Henry James
HM	*The House of Mirth,* EW
HNE	Historic New England
Houghton	Houghton Library
HRB	*Hudson River Bracketed,* EW
HS	Howard Sturgis

I Tatti	Villa I Tatti	Paris	MacMillan, *Paris 1919*
JHS	John Hugh-Smith	PL	Percy Lubbock
Letters	Lewis, *The Letters of Edith Wharton*	Portrait	Lubbock, *Portrait of Edith Wharton*
Lilly	Wharton Mss., Lilly Library	RG	Robert Grant
MB	Mary Berenson	SBC	Sarah Bradley Codman, Ogden Codman's mother
MC	Margaret "Daisy" Chanler	SF	*A Son at the Front*, EW
MF	Morton Fullerton	SN	Sally Norton
MJ	Minnie Jones	SS I	*Collected Stories, 1891–1910*, EW
MM	Beckert, *The Monied Metropolis*	SS II	*Collected Stories, 1911–1937*, EW
Mount	Edith Wharton Restoration Archives	TC	Thomas Newbold Codman
NG	Benstock, *No Gifts from Chance*	TS	*Twilight Sleep*, EW
		U Texas	Harry Ransom Humanities Research Center
NW	Nannie Wharton	VD	*The Valley of Decision*, EW
NYPL	Manuscripts and Archives New York Public Library	WB	Walter Berry
NYT	*New York Times*	WC	Winthrop Chanler
NYTBR	*New York Times Book Review*	WCB	William Crary Brownell
OC	Ogden Codman	Wright	Wright, *Edith Wharton A to Z*
Outre-Mer	Bourget, *Outre-Mer*	WT	William (Bill) Tyler

· SOURCE NOTES ·

Full citations for the sources below can be found in the bibliography.
All quotes: Edith Wharton's writings unless preceded by another source.

1. DIFFERENT

Page

1   "There was once . . .": "The
  Valley of Childish Things,"
  SS I, p. 45.

2–3   "tall splendid father," "flounced
  dresses," "mostly away," and
  "as established as the sky . . .":
  BG, p. 26.

5   "Mamma, you must go . . .":
  BG, p. 35.
  "Reading": BG, p. 36.

8   "small shrivelled bearded
  mother," "*une vieille chèvre*,"
  "*about* Mlle. Michelet's mother,"
  and "would not have said . . .":
  "Life and I," EWN, p. 1072.
  "led in with . . .": BG, p. 32.

9   "matchless track," "sport,"
  "pouring forth . . . ," and
  "tireless torrent": BG, pp. 42–43.

2. DRAWING-ROOMS ARE ALWAYS TIDY

11   "All talents . . .": FL, p. 60.
  May King Van Rensselaer,

"climb boldly . . .": quoted in
MM, 156.

13   "all the strange weeds . . .":
  A, pp. 258–59.
  "To a little girl . . .": BG,
  pp. 44–45.

13–14   "There was certainly . . .":
  BG, pp. 45–46.

14   "mind would have starved
  . . .": BG, p. 48.

14–15   "Every Sunday . . . ,"
  "unifying magic," and "in deep
  and solitary . . .": BG, p. 54.

16   "the most hideous stone
  . . .": BG, p. 55.
  "No children . . ." and "on the
  thick Turkey rug . . .": BG, p. 69.

16–17   "held literature . . . ," "stood
  in nervous dread . . . ," and
  "something between a black
  art . . .": BG, pp. 68–69.

17   "Oh, how do you do . . ." and
  "Drawing-rooms are always
  . . .": BG, p. 73.
  "starving for mental
  nourishment": EWW letter to

ET, September 3, 1938, Lilly.

19 "ringing in my ears . . .":
"Life and I," EWN, pp. 1086–87.

20 Anna Bahlmann, "Why my
dear . . .": quoted in NG, p. 31.
"Let woman beware . . .": FL, p. 2.
Lucile, by the English writer
Robert Bulwer-Lytton, was
published under the
pseudonym Owen Meredith in
1860. It remained in print in
the U.S. until 1938.

22 "twaddling romance," "a chaos
of names . . . ," and "every
character . . .": FL, pp. 113–17.
Winner analyzes Edith's
corrections on p. xvi of her
introduction.
"Who wrote these verses . . .":
quoted in Bio, Lewis, p. 32.

23 Allen Thorndike Rice, "What
you want . . .": BG, p. 75.
"shrank," "secret retreat," and
"unfitted to be either . . .":
BG, p. 75.

3. Ambition Is a Grievous Fault

24 "Nothing in life . . .": FT, p. 313.
"universe of thought" and
"enchanted region . . .": "The
Descent of Man," SS I, p. 395.

25 "The Lord High . . .": First 400,
p. 87.

26 "could meet all the people . . .":
BG, p. 77.

27 "a long cold agony . . .": BG, p. 78.
"a pink blur . . ." and "For
the rest of the winter . . .":
"Life and I," EWN, p. 1093.

28–29 Louisa Rutherford, "*I* don't
think so . . . ," "still smiles on
. . . ," and "take liberties":
quoted in Bio, Lewis, pp. 39–40.

29–30 "What were society . . .": BG,
p. 85.
"without a backward . . .": "Life
and I," EWN, p. 1094.
"I became accustomed . . .":
BG, p. 87.
"I am still haunted . . .": BG,
p. 88.
"haunted by something . . .":
BG, p. 39.

31 *Town Topics*, "Mr. Henry
Stevens . . .": quoted in Bio,
Lewis, p. 44.
"impossible . . .": EWW letter
to ET, October 16, 1938, Lilly.

31–32 *Town Topics*, "the marriage
of . . .": quoted in Bio, Lewis,
p. 45.

32 Helen Rhinelander, "Mrs. S
behaved . . .": quoted in Bio,
Lewis, p. 45.
NYT obituary, April 4, 1895,
"an ambitious woman . . .":
quoted in Astor, p. 208.
Newport Daily News, "The only
reason . . .": quoted in Bio,
Lewis, p. 45.

34 "the Love of all my life": EW
daily diary, October 12, 1927,
Beinecke.

4 . SUNSHINE IN THE HOUSE

35 "She had been bored . . .": HM,
p. 23.
"To talk with him . . .": "The
Letters," SS I, p. 865.

36 "shell . . . with nothing . . . ,"
"chill from within," and
"lowering the temperature": PL,
Portrait, pp. 229–30.
"a great deal . . ." and "a fleeting
hint . . .": BG, p. 107.
"the fond and foolish . . .":
"Descent of Man," SS I, p. 408.

37 "To have been loved . . .":
The Touchstone, SS I, p. 164.
"sunshine in the house": EWW
letter to ET, December 8, 1938,
Lilly.

38 newspaper reporter, "were on
hand . . .": quoted in Bio, Lewis,
p. 42.

39 "expected there would have
been": *Town Topics*, quoted in
Bio, Lewis, p. 51.

40 "seized with such . . . ,"
"what being married . . . ," "I'm
afraid . . . ," "You've seen . . . ,"
"Well, then . . . ," and "For
heaven's sake . . .": "Life and I,"
EWN, pp. 1087–88.

40-41 "startled puzzled . . . ," "the large

double-bed," "terror," and
"resigned smiles . . .": "The Old
Maid," EWN, p. 377.

42 "I wouldn't . . ." and "No, if I
were you . . .": Teddy Wharton,
quoted in Portrait, p. 22.

43 "the chief industry" and "the
business of granting . . .": May
King Van Rensselaer, quoted in
First 400, p. 184.
"confused din of dancing . . ."
and "crushing into . . .": George
William Curtis, quoted in First
400, p. 185.
"an occult . . .": quoted in NG,
p. 96.
"My new friend . . .": BG, p. 94.

44 "heavy carriage . . .": BG, p. 102.
"My dear . . .": Egerton
Winthrop, quoted in BG, p. 103.

45 "With the open road . . .": PL,
Portrait, p. 109.

47 "I would give . . .": BG, p. 96.
"Do you really?" and "All right
. . .": Teddy Wharton, quoted in
BG, p. 98.
"the greatest step forward . . .":
BG, p. 98.
"grasping the folds . . .": CV,
p. 119.
"it was useless . . .": CV, p. 51.
"we sat on the bridge . . .": CV,
p. 92.
"The early established rule . . .":
CV, p. 173.

48 "sat in the sunshine . . ." and "we went in . . .": CV, pp. 174–75.
"difficult and wonderful": BG, p. 100.

49 "I shall never forget . . .": BG, p. 109.
"He not only . . .": BG, p. 109.
"We cannot often . . .": ELB letter to EW, May 26, 1890, Firestone.

50 Caroline Astor, "We have no right . . .": quoted in Astor, p. 272.

51 "an ugly wooden house . . .": BG, p. 106.
"wobbly velvet-covered tables . . .": BG, p. 107.

5. NEW WRITER WHO COUNTS

52 "Sometimes I feel . . .": "The Introducers," SS I, p. 549.

52–53 "The American spirit . . ." and "On the floors . . .": Paul Bourget, Outre-Mer, pp. 47–49.

53 "establish an artificial . . ." and "born to social station . . .": Paul Bourget, Outre-Mer, pp. 54–55.

54 "intellectual tomboy . . .": Paul Bourget, Outre-Mer, p. 93.
"one ignorance . . .": Paul Bourget, Outre-Mer, p. 94.
"I need hardly say . . .": letter to ELB, November 25, 1893, Firestone.

55 "creaked, and he always . . .": "The Fulness of Life," SS I, p. 15.

"I have sometimes . . . ," "the innermost room . . . ," and "the soul sits . . .": "The Fulness of Life," SS I, p. 14.
"I seem to have fallen . . .": letter to ELB, March 26, 1894, Firestone.
"If Messrs. Scribners still . . .": letter to ELB, July 30, 1894, Firestone.

56 "Since I last wrote . . ." and "waif": letter to ELB, December 14, 1895, Firestone.
"Finding that we had . . .": BG, p. 107.

58 "I literally could not write . . .": BG, p. 107.
"I regret very much . . ." letter to OC, June 1897, HNE.

58–59 "I remember shyly . . .": BG, p. 108.

59 "large insight": WB, quoted in NG, p. 87.
"small town-houses" and "exquisite discomfort": quoted in Bio, Lewis, p. 79.

60 "I hate to think so . . .": Teddy Wharton, quoted in NG, p. 88.
"there was nothing . . ." and "facts were . . .": "The Pelican," SS I, p. 77.
"He followed . . .": BG, pp. 112–13.

61 "one long shriek": letter to ELB, July 10, 1898, Firestone.

"New Writer . . ." and "We have
seen . . .": Harry Thurston Peck,
quoted in NG, p. 99.
"At last I had groped . . .": BG,
p. 119.

61–62   "Her work was not . . ." and "Her
books, growing . . .": PL,
Portrait, p. 60.

63   "I can see her . . .": GL, quoted in
Portrait, p. 76.
"This is what everybody . . .":
James Bain, quoted in BG, p. 123.
"Any one walking along . . .": BG,
p. 113.
"who were thinking and creating"
and "wearisome frivolity": BG,
p. 123.

64   "till our return . . .": letter to
WCB, September 26, 1889,
Firestone.
"all that sogginess": WB, quoted
in Bio, Lewis, p. 94.
"Don't, don't . . ." and "I do
wish . . .": WB, quoted in NG,
p. 108.
"never never well land": WB,
quoted in NG, p. 114.

65   "The truth is . . .": letter to OC,
August 1, 1900, HNE.
"The thing has taken . . .": letter
to WCB, August 19, 1900,
Firestone.
"Don't think me . . .":
letter to WCB, November 7,
1900, Firestone.

6. A REPUBLIC OF THE SPIRIT

67   "She sought in vain . . .": VD, vol.
II, p. 81.

67–68   "I applaud . . . ," "a little *hard*,"
and "Do, some day . . .": HJ
letter to EW, October 26, 1900,
Beinecke.

69   "Dear Madam . . .": BG, p. 126.
"to a shadow" and "fussing": OC
letter to SBC, February 17, 1901,
HNE.
"Teddy Wharton seems . . .": OC
letter to SBC, December 19,
1902, HNE.
"dead right . . .": WB, quoted in
NG, p. 119.
"in name only": OC letter to SBC,
January 10, 1902, HNE.
"story about the Sloanes . . .": OC
letter to SBC, July 1, 1901, HNE.

70   "I excessively hate . . .": letter to
SN, January 24, 1902, Beinecke.
"an impertinence": letter to WCB,
December 25, 1901, Firestone.
"earnestly, tenderly . . .": HJ
letter to EW, August 17, 1902,
Beinecke.

71   *Really it is a pity . . .*": OC letter
to SBC, October 8, 1902, HNE.

72   "content with nothing less . . .":
Mrs. Gordon Bell, quoted in
Portrait, p. 27.
"with respectful severity": GL,
quoted in Portrait, p. 84.
"with her wise old . . ." and

"everywhere": PL, Portrait, p. 84.

72–73 "What an amusing . . .": Daniel Berkeley Updike, quoted in Portrait, p. 20.

73 "abundant" and "sparkling": RG, quoted in Portrait, p. 46.

74 "I am bothered . . .": quoted in Bio, Lewis, p. 114.

"as he will probably . . .": OC letter to SBC, December 19, 1902, HNE.

"never enjoyed any . . .": BG, p. 136.

"The day of the motor ": BG, p. 135.

"Most of the places . . .": BG, p. 136

74–75 "put behind" and "I climbed proudly . . .": BG, p. 137.

75 "more acutely . . ." and "wretched": letter to SN, June 5, 1903, Beinecke.

"Her life was . . .": Gustave Flaubert, quoted in Bio, Lewis, p. 123.

76 "I mustn't omit . . .": HJ letter to MJ, June 9, 1903, quoted in EWHJ, p. 88.

"a motor-car . . .": quoted in Bio, Lewis, p. 128.

"With the proceeds . . .": HJ, quoted in Portrait, p. 68.

77 "it had been . . ." and "While others . . .": PL, Portrait, pp. 67–68.

"lived in terror . . . ," "thin worn turf . . . ," "unkempt flower . . . ," "white-panelled . . . ," "old prints," and "crowded book-cases": BG, pp. 244–45.

"little sputtering . . .": letter to SN, July 12, 1904, Beinecke.

77–78 "for in those days . . .": BG, p. 152.

78 "grandly calm": quoted in PL, Portrait, p. 85.

79 "the severest test . . ." and "My last page . . .": BG, p. 208.

80 "a negative hero": quoted in Bio, Lewis, p. 155.

82 "persecuted": letter to CS, October 31, 1905, Firestone.

"I have just finished . . .": *Detroit Post* article, quoted in NG, p. 155.

"It is a very remarkable book . . .": WC, quoted in Bio, Lewis, p. 153.

"New York society is still . . .": letter to William Roscoe Thayer, November 11, 1905, Houghton.

"We are sailing . . .": letter to SN, March 1, 1906, Beinecke.

83 "the best school of talk . . .": FW, p. 117.

"small thin woman" and "always eager . . .": BG, p. 265.

"a book-collector . . ." and "I've just read . . .": BG, pp. 266–67.

84 "This—this, my dear Cook . . .":

HJ, quoted in BG, p. 241. HJ
misquotes line 1 from John
Milton's poem "Samson
Agonistes": "A little onward
lend thy guiding hand."

"In short my good man . . .": HJ,
quoted in BG, p. 243.

84–85   "reluctance to repair . . .": BG,
p. 228.

85   "weedy lawn . . ." and "not too
successful . . .": BG, p. 225.

"white-panelled walls . . . ,"
"profound chintz . . . ," and
"drollest, kindest . . .": BG,
p. 225.

"indolent and unambitious" and
"his social gifts . . .": BG, p. 230.

"in the shade": PL, Portrait, p. 9.

"like a sort of concerto . . .": PL,
Portrait, p. 5.

"here, in such talk . . ." PL,
Portrait, p. 4.

"the game of conversation . . .":
PL, Portrait, p. 56.

86   "a meteor from overseas . . . ,"
"old and easy . . . ," "at home
. . . ," and "he seemed . . .": PL,
Portrait, p. 72.

"an answering mind": VD, vol. II,
p. 81.

87   "a republic of the spirit": HM,
p. 55.

7. WYCH-HAZEL

88   "No one had ever known . . .":

"Atrophy," SS II, p. 436.

"The great . . .": HJ, quoted in
Wright, p. 134.

89   "There was a curious . . .": EW
letter to SN, January 24, 1907,
Beinecke.

89–90   "I soon became . . .": BG, p. 268.

90   "two champions likely . . .": FW,
p. 23.

"never go out . . .": BG, p. 267.

91   "I know I shall . . ." and "My
three weeks . . .": HJ, quoted in
EWHJ, pp. 133–34.

"very intelligent, but . . .": letter
to SN, April 21, 1907, Beinecke.

"find-able at . . .": EW letter to
MF, June 1, 1907, U Texas.

92   "If you had not . . .": Love Diary,
October 29, 1907, Lilly.

"stole up . . . ," "Was its name
. . . ," and "You hurt me . . .":
Love Diary, February 21 and 22,
1908, Lilly.

93   "I have found . . .": letter to MF,
February 1908, U Texas.

"I'm so afraid . . .": letter to
MF, March 1908, U Texas.

95   "I am deeply . . .": HJ, quoted
in EWHJ, pp. 153–54.

"I am sleeping better . . .":
letter to SN, November 18,
1908, Beinecke.

96   "general eagle-pounces . . ." and
"Angel of Devastation": HJ letter
to GL, May 4, 1909, Houghton.

"The letters survive . . .": EW
letter to MF, December 31,
1909, U Texas.

97   "seems *perfectly* well . . .": NW
letter to EW, September 20,
1909, Beinecke.

97–98   "I am not free . . .": FPK letter to
EW, December 19, 1909,
Beinecke.

98   "Wonderful . . . ," "the low wide
bed . . . ," "the wide flair of cities
. . . ," and "a harbourless
wind-bitten shore . . .":
"Terminus," Beinecke.
"Terminus" did not appear in
print until 1975.
"It is impossible . . .": letter to
MF, late summer, 1909,
U Texas.

8. STORM AND SORROW

101   "It was one thing . . .": TS, p. 184.
"And if you knew . . .": letter to
MF, May 1910, U Texas.

102   "the storm . . .": HJ, quoted in
Bio, Lewis, p. 302.
"Electric fans . . ." and "off again
. . .": BG, pp. 187–88.

103   "Good God, what a woman . . .":
HJ, quoted in BG, p. 189.
"utterly quarrelsome . . .": HJ
letter to HS, August 17, 1911,
Houghton.

104   "about as bad . . .": letter to MJ,
September 23, 1911, Beinecke.

"Teddy looks splendidly . . .":
letter to GL, July 18, 1911,
Beinecke.
"There was no way out . . .": EF,
p. 55.

104–5   "cruel story" and "something
very much finer . . .": quoted in
NYTBR, August 11, 1911.

106   "shock-absorber": NG, p. 262.
"'Learning French' . . .": letter to
MF, not dated, U Texas.
"wailing for me . . .": letter to BB,
March 14, 1912, I Tatti.

107   "Mr. Scribner . . . is mortally
hurt . . .": letter to MF, June 27,
1912, U Texas.
"Do you think . . .": letter to MF,
June 25, 1912, U Texas.
"I count on you for dinner . . .":
letter to MF, August 12, 1912,
U Texas.

108   "out of *its* clutches": letter to GL,
August 19, 1912, Beinecke.
"quite the finest thing": HJ letter
to EW, December 1912,
Beinecke.
"Only *please* don't . . .": letter
to BB, November 23, 1912, I
Tatti.
"If only my work . . .": letter to
JHS, November 25, 1912,
Beinecke.

108–9   "under the rule . . .": letter to
GL, February 8, 1913,
Beinecke.

109 "the dearest of brothers . . .":
letter to BB, August 23, 1922, I
Tatti.
"damned well rid . . ." and
"improper relations . . .": Teddy
Wharton, quoted in OC letters
to SBC, May 5 and February 20,
1913, HNE.
"anemic" and "much use . . .":
OC letter to SBC, June 24, 1913,
HNE.

110 "leaf by leaf": quoted in Bio,
Lewis, p. 339.
"rather down . . . ," "harlot,"
"unedifying condition . . . ," and
"have made them rather . . .": OC
letter to SBC, December 7, 1913,
HNE.

111 "spoiled several . . ." and
"nervous with jealousy": MB
letter to GS, January 1914,
I Tatti.

112 "Fasten with all your might . . .":
quoted in NG, p. 290.
"a pale demon," "four black
gnome-like . . . ," "Here's
your year . . . ," and
"limp black squirming
things": quoted in Bio, Lee,
p. 444.
"best and most comprehensive
. . .": EW letter to CS,
February 23, 1914, Houghton.
"Are you sure . . .": quoted in Bio,
Lee, p. 444.

9. THE WORST OF DOING GOOD

113 "France, his France . . .": *The
Marne*, SS II, p. 264.

114 "gave little thought . . .": BG,
p. 338.
"glorious hours . . ." and
"Spain in July . . .": letter to BB,
July 26, 1914, I Tatti.
"The air seemed full . . .": FF, p. 4.
"air was thundery . . ." and
"whole incalculable weight . . .":
FF, pp. 6–7.

115 "A huge break . . . ," "The War
Office . . . ": FF, p. 9.
"the army of midsummer . . . ,"
"resounding emptiness . . . ,"
and "the gradual paralysis . . .":
FF, pp. 12–13.

115–16 "DETAINED IN PARIS . . .": cable to
CS, August 4, 1914, Firestone.

116 "there was an ardour . . .": BG,
p. 341.
"civilized & big-treed . . .": HJ
quoted in End, p. 9.
"I hardly know . . .": letter to SN,
September 2, 1914, Beinecke.
"There began to be rumours . . .":
BG, p. 343.

117 "My co-workers . . .": letter to
SN, September 2, 1914,
Beinecke.
"I am simply sick . . .": letter to
BB, September 3, 1914, I Tatti.

118 "We now have . . .": letter to SN,
September 27, 1914, Beinecke.

"the blessed drug of hard work":
BG, p. 343.

118–19 "You must forgive . . .": letter to
BB, September 30, 1914, I Tatti.

119 "Walter tries to pretend . . .":
quoted in End, p. 41.
"measured by the shadow . . ."
and "people who stand . . .": FF,
pp. 34–35.

120 "friends and strangers" and "as
untiringly as those . . .": BG,
p. 350.
"could stimulate . . .": PL,
Portrait, p. 127.
"My husband and I . . .": ET,
quoted in BG, p. 348.

121 "a tottering house of cards . . .":
BG, pp. 348–49.

122 "little widows": ET, Report on
War Charities, Lilly.

123 "All the Belgians in Paris . . .":
WB, quoted in Bio, Lewis, p. 379.
"not very proud . . .": quoted in
NG, p. 313.
"four rows of wooden cots . . .":
FF, p. 68.
"The women wailed . . .": FF,
p. 70.

124 "things have killed it . . .":
quoted in NG, p. 313.
"literary salad . . .": letter to BB,
July 24, 1915, I Tatti.
"What was the war of 1870 . . .":
Paul Bourget, quoted in BH,
p. 68.

125 "condemned . . . by doddering
. . .": HJ letter to EW, March 5,
1915, Beinecke.
"You're magnificent . . .": HJ,
quoted in EWHJ, p. 207.
"I am so struck . . .": HJ, quoted
in BH, p. 118.
"There is nothing to do now
. . .": quoted in NG, p. 321; "all
that mighty heart" is from
Wordsworth's "Upon
Westminster Bridge" (slightly
misquoted: original reads "is
lying still").
"He died without suffering . . .":
letter to André Gide, March 5,
1916 (translation), Letters,
p. 372.
"Everything I did . . .": BG, pp.
356–57.
"The worst of doing good . . .":
quoted in End, p. 42.

126 "enormous and varied work . . .":
Figaro article, April 8, 1916,
quoted in Bio, Lewis, p. 386.
"for your attachment . . .":
workwomen, quoted in Bio,
Lewis, p. 387.
"I do not remember . . .": BG,
p. 356.

127 "I want very much . . .": letter to
WT, November 11, 1916, Lilly.

128 "For the last ten days . . .":
quoted in End, p. 110.
"The cold is still grim": letter to

BB, February 9, 1917, I Tatti.

129 "The chief interest . . .": letter to
AG, March 23, 1918, Garrett.
"The immovable war . . .": PL,
Portrait, p. 134.

10. I WANT TO GO HOME

131 "You ought to buy it . . .":
"Kerfol," SS II, p. 89.
"hushed November day," "The
quarter I lived in . . . ," and "one
after another . . .": BG,
pp. 359–60.

132 "Before we get through . . .": an
American, quoted in Paris,
p. 14.
"It has taken days . . .": letter to
BB, January 27, 1919, I Tatti.

133 "We moved in . . ." and "faithful
household": letter to MJ,
December 26, 1920, Beinecke.

134 "a belated essay . . .": reviewer
for the *Bookman* (vol. 65,
p. 46), quoted in Shari
Benstock's introduction to SF,
p. viii.

135 "laughs at the . . . tyranny . . ."
and "she has painted . . .":
Vernon L. Parrington in *Pacific
Review*, June 1921, quoted in
appendix to A, p. 357.
"old landmarks . . .": A, p. 338.

136 "You bring back . . .": MJ letter to
EW, December 19, 1919,
Beinecke.

"We are the last . . .": WB, BG,
p. 369.
"It is one of the best . . .":
William Lyon Phelps, from
NYTBR, October 17, 1920,
quoted in A (appendix), p. 364.

137 "a turgid welter . . .": letter to
BB, January 6, 1923, I Tatti.

137–38 "I am really turning into . . .":
letter to MC, June 9, 1925,
Beinecke.

138 "a deplorable example . . .":
letter to William Gerhardie,
October 7, 1922, U Texas.
"touched" and "the literary
equivalent . . .": letter to
F. Scott Fitzgerald, June 8, 1925,
Firestone.
"To tea . . . Scott Fitzgerald . . .":
quoted in Bio, Lee, p. 622.

139 "wondering and wondering,"
"*hadn't*—for it . . . ," and "I've
never 'wondered' . . .": WB
letter to EW, February 25, 1923,
Beinecke.
"stuttering paralytic": WB,
quoted in NG, p. 399.
"dreadful devouring quality":
ET journal, Lilly.

141 "dear" and "The Love of all my
life . . .": EW's daily diary,
October 12, 1927, Beinecke.
"I feel totally rudderless":
letter to BB, October 27, 1927,
I Tatti.

"I perceive now that I . . .": letter
to JHS, October 15, 1927,
Beinecke.

"At my age . . .": letter to MB,
January 11, 1928, I Tatti.

142   "sunshine in the house": EWW
letter to ET, December 8, 1938,
Lilly.

142–43 "You will go back . . .": letter to
RG, February 10, 1928,
Beinecke. Teddy Wharton was
probably afflicted with bipolar
disorder.

144   "into another sphere": Nicky
Mariano, collected letters of
Percy Lubbock, Beinecke.

145   "the greatest proof . . .": HRB,
p. 444.

"woes and privations . . .": MJ,
quoted in NG, p. 431.

"The farther I have penetrated
. . .": quoted in NG, p. 431.

146   "this wonderful adventure . . .":
letter to MB, October 11, 1936,
I Tatti.

146–47 "full of oases . . .": letter to BB,
April 9, 1937, I Tatti.

147   "She no longer . . .": BB, quoted

in Bio, Lewis, p. 495.

149   "We really communicated . . .":
letter to WT, May 16, 1937, Lilly.

"This will teach you . . .": OC
letter to TC, June 5, 1937,
HNE.

"We lived through . . .": ET
journal, Lilly.

"Oh, up to about . . .": WT letter
to PL, November 7, 1947, Lilly.

"He enjoyed life . . .": quoted in
ET journal, Lilly.

"Impulses and emotions . . .":
quoted in ET journal, Lilly.

150   "I want to go home . . .": quoted
in ET journal, Lilly.

"sovereign mind . . ." and "It's all
right . . .": quoted in ET journal,
Lilly.

"Now it's all over . . .": Alfred
White, quoted in Dwight, p. 282.

AFTERWORD. THE GIST OF ME

151   "What's the use . . .": A, p. 336.

"For My Biographer": quoted in
Bio, Lewis, p. xi.

"find the gist of me": EW diary,
Beinecke.

· BIBLIOGRAPHY ·

ARCHIVES

Alice Warder Garrett Archives, Evergreen House Foundation, at Evergreen House, Johns Hopkins University, Baltimore, Md.

Charles Scribner's Sons Archive, Scribner Room, Department of Rare Books and Special Collections, Firestone Library, Princeton University, Princeton, N.J.

Edith Wharton Collection, Yale Collection of American Literature, Beinecke Rare Book and Manuscript Library, Yale University, New Haven, Conn.

Edith Wharton Restoration Archives, The Mount, Lenox, Mass.

Harry Ransom Humanities Research Center, University of Texas at Austin, Tex.

Historic New England (formerly Society for the Preservation of New England Antiquities), Boston, Mass.

Houghton Library, Harvard University, Cambridge, Mass.

Villa I Tatti, Florence, Italy. Harvard University Center for Italian Renaissance Studies.

Wharton Mss. and Appleton-Century Mss.,
Lilly Library, Indiana University, Bloomington, Ind.

GENERAL SOURCES

Barnes, Nat. *The Etiquette of Motoring.* East Grinstead, Sussex, England: Copper Beech Publishing, 1997.

Beckert, Sven. *The Monied Metropolis: New York City and the Consolidation of the American Bourgeoisie, 1850–1896.* New York: Cambridge University Press, 2001.

Bell, Millicent. *Edith Wharton & Henry James: The Story of Their Friendship.* New York: George Braziller, 1965.

Benstock, Shari. *No Gifts from Chance: A Biography of Edith Wharton.* New York: Charles Scribner's Sons, 1994.

Bourget, Paul. *Outre-Mer: Impressions of America.* New York: Charles Scribner's Sons, 1895.

Downey, Fairfax. *Portrait of an Era as Drawn by C. D. Gibson.* New York: Charles Scribner's Sons, 1936.

Dwight, Eleanor. *Edith Wharton: An Extraordinary Life.* New York: Harry N. Abrams, 1994.

Flink, James J. *America Adopts the Automobile, 1895–1910.* Cambridge, Mass.: MIT Press, 1970.

Fromkin, David. *Europe's Last Summer: Who Started the Great War in 1914?* New York: Alfred A. Knopf, 2004.

Hammack, David C. *Power and Society: Greater New York at the Turn of the Century.* New York: Columbia University Press, 1987.

Homberger, Eric. *Mrs. Astor's New York: Money and Social Power in a Gilded Age.* New Haven: Yale University Press, 2002.

Horne, Alistair. *The Price of Glory: Verdun 1916.* London: Penguin Books, 1993.

——. *Seven Ages of Paris.* New York: Alfred A. Knopf, 2002.

Howard, Maureen, ed. *Edith Wharton: Collected Stories, 1891–1910.* New York: Library of America, 2001.

——. *Edith Wharton: Collected Stories, 1911–1937.* New York: Library of America, 2001.

Keegan, John. *The First World War.* New York: Alfred A. Knopf, 1999.

Lee, Hermione. *Edith Wharton.* New York: Alfred A. Knopf, 2007.

Lewis, R. W. B. *Edith Wharton: A Biography.* New York: Harper & Row, 1975.

——, and Nancy Lewis, eds. *The Letters of Edith Wharton.* New York: Charles Scribner's Sons, 1988.

Lubbock, Percy. *Portrait of Edith Wharton.* New York: D. Appleton-Century, 1947.

MacMillan, Margaret. *Paris 1919: Six Months That Changed the World.* New York: Random House, 2002.

Mainwaring, Marion. *The Mysteries of Paris: The Quest for Morton Fullerton.* Hanover, N.H.: University Press of New England, 2001.

Patterson, Jerry E. *The First Four Hundred: Mrs. Astor's New York in the Gilded Age.* New York: Rizzoli, 2000.

Price, Alan. *The End of the Age of Innocence: Edith Wharton and the First World War.* New York: St. Martin's, 1996.

Wharton, Edith. *The Age of Innocence,* ed. Michael Nowlin. Toronto: Broadview Press, 2002.

——. *A Backward Glance.* New York: Touchstone/Simon & Schuster, 1998.

——, ed. *The Book of the Homeless.* New York: Charles Scribner's Sons, 1916.

——. *The Cruise of the Vanadis.* New York: Rizzoli, 2004.

——. *Ethan Frome,* ed. Kristin O. Lauer and Cynthia Griffin Wolff. New York: W. W. Norton, 1995.

——. *Fighting France: From Dunkerque to Belfort.* New York: Charles Scribner's Sons, 1919.

——. *French Ways and Their Meaning.* Lee, Mass.: Berkshire House Publishers, 1997.

———. *The Fruit of the Tree.* Boston: North-eastern University Press, 2000.

———. *The Gods Arrive.* New York: Charles Scribner's Sons, 1932.

———. *The House of Mirth.* New York: W. W. Norton, 1990.

———. *Hudson River Bracketed.* New York: Charles Scribner's Sons, 1985.

———. *A Son at the Front.* DeKalb: Northern Illinois University Press, 1995.

———. *Twilight Sleep.* New York: Simon & Schuster, 1997.

———. *The Valley of Decision.* New York: Charles Scribner's Sons, 1902.

Winner, Viola Hopkins, ed. *Fast and Loose; and, The Buccaneers.* Charlottes-ville: University of Virginia Press, 1993.

Wolff, Cynthia Griffin, ed. *Edith Wharton: Novellas and Other Writings.* New York: Library of America, 1990.

Wright, Sarah Bird. *Edith Wharton A to Z: The Essential Guide to the Life and Work.* New York: Facts on File, 1998.

· WORKS BY EDITH WHARTON ·

There have been many editions of Edith Wharton's work through the years. The original publishers and publication dates are listed below. The specific editions I quoted from in this biography can be found in the bibliography.

1878   *Verses;* privately printed by C. E. Hammett, Jr., Newport, R.I.

1897   *The Decoration of Houses* with Ogden Codman, Jr., nonfiction; Scribner's.

1899   *The Greater Inclination,* short stories; Scribner's.

1900   *The Touchstone,* novella; Scribner's.

1901   *Crucial Instances,* short stories; Scribner's.

1902   *The Valley of Decision,* novel; Scribner's.

1903   *Sanctuary,* novella; Scribner's.

1904   *The Descent of Man and Other Stories,* short stories; Scribner's.

1904   *Italian Villas and Their Gardens,* nonfiction; Century.

1905   *Italian Backgrounds,* nonfiction; Scribner's.

1905   *The House of Mirth,* novel; Scribner's.

1907   *Madame de Treymes,* novella; Scribner's.

1907   *The Fruit of the Tree,* novel; Scribner's.

1908   *A Motor-Flight Through France,* nonfiction; Scribner's.

1908   *The Hermit and the Wild Woman and Other Stories,* short stories; Scribner's.

1909   *Artemis to Actaeon and Other Verse,* poetry; Scribner's.

1910   *Tales of Men and Ghosts,* short stories; Scribner's.

1911   *Ethan Frome,* novella; Scribner's.

1912   *The Reef,* novel; D. Appleton.

1913   *The Custom of the Country,* novel; Scribner's.

1915   *Fighting France: From Dunkerque to Belfort,* nonfiction; Scribner's.

1916   *Xingu and Other Stories,* short stories; Scribner's.

1916   *The Book of the Homeless,* collected essays; Scribner's.

1917   *Summer,* novella; D. Appleton.

1918   *The Marne*, novella; D. Appleton.

1919   *French Ways and Their Meaning*, nonfiction; D. Appleton.

1920   *The Age of Innocence*, novel; D. Appleton.

1920   *In Morocco*, nonfiction; Scribner's.

1922   *The Glimpses of the Moon*, novel; D. Appleton.

1923   *A Son at the Front*, novel; Scribner's.

1924   *False Dawn*, novella; D. Appleton.

1924   *The Old Maid*, novella; D. Appleton.

1924   *The Spark*, novella; D. Appleton.

1924   *New Year's Day*, novella, D. Appleton.

1925   *The Mother's Recompense*, novella; D. Appleton.

1925   *The Writing of Fiction*, nonfiction; Scribner's.

1926   *Here and Beyond*, short stories; D. Appleton.

1926   *Twelve Poems*, poetry; London: Medici Society.

1927   *Twilight Sleep*, novel; D. Appleton.

1928   *The Children*, novel; D. Appleton.

1929   *Hudson River Bracketed*, novel; D. Appleton.

1930   *Certain People*, short stories; D. Appleton.

1932   *The Gods Arrive* (sequel to *Hudson River Bracketed*), novel; D. Appleton.

1933   *Human Nature*, short stories; D. Appleton.

1934   *A Backward Glance*, memoir; D. Appleton.

1936   *The World Over*, short stories; D. Appleton.

1937   *Ghosts*, short stories; D. Appleton.

Published Posthumously

1938   *The Buccaneers*, unfinished novel; D. Appleton-Century.

1977   *Fast and Loose: A Novelette*, by "David Olivieri." Viola Hopkins Winner, ed.; University Press of Virginia.

FILM ADAPTATIONS OF EDITH WHARTON'S WORKS

1918   *The House of Mirth*, Metro; directed by Albert Capellani; silent, now lost.

1923   *The Glimpses of the Moon*, Paramount; directed by Allan Dwan; silent, now lost.

1924	*The Age of Innocence*, Warner Brothers; directed by Wesley Ruggles; silent, now lost.
1929	*The Marriage Playground* (based on *The Children*), Paramount; directed by Lothar Mendes.
1934	*The Age of Innocence*, RKO Radio; directed by Philip Moeller, stars Irene Dunne and John Boles.
1935	*Strange Wives* (based on the short story "Bread upon the Waters"), Universal; directed by Richard Thorpe; now lost.
1939	*The Old Maid*, Warner Brothers; directed by Edmund Goulding, stars Bette Davis and George Brent; available on videocassette.
1960	*Ethan Frome*, for television; directed by Alex Segal, stars Sterling Hayden and Julie Harris; may be viewed at the Museum of Broadcasting in New York City.
1981	*The House of Mirth*, for television; directed by Adrian Hall, stars Geraldine Chaplin and William Atherton.
1981	*Summer*, for television; directed by Dezso Magyar, stars Diane Lane and Michael Ontkean.
1983	*The Lady's Maid's Bell*, for television; directed by John Glenister, stars Joanna David and June Brown.
1983	*Afterward*, for television; directed by Simon Langton, stars Kate Harper and Michael J. Shannon.
1983	*Bewitched*, for television; directed by John Gorrie, stars Eileen Atkins and Alfred Burke.
1990	*The Children*, Isolde Films; directed by Tony Palmer, stars Ben Kingsley, Kim Novak, and Geraldine Chaplin; limited release on videocassette.
1993	*Ethan Frome*, Miramax; directed by John Madden, stars Liam Neeson and Patricia Arquette; available on videocassette.
1993	*The Age of Innocence*, Columbia Pictures; directed by Martin Scorsese, stars Daniel Day-Lewis, Michelle Pfeiffer, Winona Ryder, and Geraldine Chaplin.
1995	*The Buccaneers*, for television; directed by Philip Saville, stars Cheri Lunghi and Carla Gugino.
2000	*The House of Mirth*, Sony Picture Classics; directed by Terence Davies, stars Gillian Anderson and Dan Aykroyd.

[Note: Except for the last entry for 2000, The House of Mirth, these films are listed in Wright's Edith Wharton A to Z, *pp. 288–92.]*

· PICTURE CREDITS ·

AC and World of Stock: 128

AP Images: 138

Archives of the Episcopal Diocese of New York: 2

Astor family papers, Manuscripts and Archives Division, The New York Public Library, Astor, Lenox, and Tilden Foundations: 12 (bottom)

Clifton Waller Barrett Library of American Literature, Special Collections, University of Virginia Library: 23

Historic Landmarks Foundation of Indiana, West Baden Springs Program: 106

Historic New England: 56

Isabella Stewart Gardner Museum, Boston: 54

Library of Congress Prints and Photographs Division: 12 (top), 46

The Lilly Library, Indiana University, Bloomington, Indiana: 4 (bottom), 14, 19, 21 (both), 33, 42, 73, 78, 90, 99, 129, 136, 142, 143

The Mount Archives: 3 (both), 4 (top), 5

Picture Collection, The New York Public Library, Astor, Lenox and Tilden Foundations: 15, 26, 28

Sophia Smith Collection, Smith College: 83

Yale Collection of American Literature, Beinecke Rare Book and Manuscript Library: iv, 6, 9, 16, 25, 29, 30, 36, 39, 45, 50, 57 (both), 59, 60, 62, 65, 68, 71, 75, 76, 80, 81, 82, 84, 86, 89, 93, 94, 97, 102, 103, 105, 108, 115, 118, 121, 122, 124, 127, 135, 137, 140, 144, 147, 148, 153

· ACKNOWLEDGMENTS ·

I would like to thank the following individuals, agencies, and institutions for permission to quote from materials in their possession: the Edith Wharton Collection, Yale Collection of American Literature, Beinecke Rare Book and Manuscript Library, Yale University; the Berenson Archive, the Harvard University Center for Italian Renaissance Studies, Villa I Tatti, Florence, Italy; Houghton Library, Harvard University; the Lilly Library, Indiana University, Bloomington, Indiana; Charles Scribners' Sons Archives, Manuscripts Division, Department of Rare Books and Special Collections, Princeton University Library; Historic New England, formerly the Society for the Preservation of New England Antiquities, Boston; the Harry Ransom Humanities Research Center, University of Texas at Austin; the Watkins/Loomis Agency; Clifton Waller Barrett Library of American Literature, Special Collections, University of Virginia Library; Alice Warder Garrett Archives, Johns Hopkins University.

In addition, special thanks to the following people: David Dashiell, Susan Wissler, Anthony Cafaro, and Molly McFall at the Mount in Lenox, Massachusetts; Arthur Ling, Saundra Taylor, Zach Downey, and Cherry Williams at Indiana University; my research assistants, Emmy Chang at Princeton University, Stephanie Rosen at the University of Texas at Austin, and John Ulrich at Harvard University; Fiorella Superbi at Villa I Tatti; and Amanda Pennelly of Watkins/Loomis, who courageously fielded a barrage of questions.

I'm especially grateful to those who slogged through early versions of the manuscript, some of them more than once: the members of my Cincinnati writers' group (Andrea Cheng, Cathryn Long, Sally Derby Miller, Dave Richardson, Mary Ann Rosswurm, Linda Sanders, Linda Leopold Strauss, and Kathy Wiechman), Lynda Jackson, Peggy Schafir, Barbara Mays, and Carolyn Yoder. Thanks also to Greg Logan for his help with the photos.

Thanks to my editor, Dinah Stevenson, and her hyperactive green pencil.

And a last thank-you to my husband, Carl, who now knows Edith Wharton almost as well as I do.

· INDEX ·

Note: Page numbers in **bold type** refer to illustrations.

Academy of Music, New York, **26**, 38, 46

Alcott, Louisa May, *Little Women*, 6–7

American Hostels for Refugees, 120, 121, **121**

American Red Cross, 128–29

Astor, Caroline, and New York Society, 11–12, **12**, 25, 26, 38, 46, 49–50, 134

Atlantic Monthly, 23, 48, 110

Bahlmann, Anna, 14, 18, 20, 61, 80, 141, 149

Bar Harbor, Maine, social life in, 28, 34

Bedlow, Henry, 8

Berenson, Bernard, 99–100, **99**, 110, 144
   and Edith's death, 150
   Edith's letters to, 106, 137, 141, 146–47
   Edith's wartime letters to, 114, 117, 119, 123, 125, 128, 132
   and Edith's writing, 108
   and Tyler, 120–21

Berenson, Mary, 99, 100, 111, 141, 146

Berry, Walter Van Rensselaer, 34, **36**, **103**
   and *The Decoration of Houses*, 58–59
   and Edith's car, **115**
   Edith's friendship with, 63, 87, 90, 95, 100, 101–2, 109, 111, 139, 143, **143**, 149, 151

Berry, Walter Van Rensselaer (*cont.*)
   and Edith's writing, 58–59, 60–61, 67, 82, 107, 136, 142
   in Europe, 105–6, 111, 112, 113–14, 134, 139
   grave of, 150
   illness and death of, 139, 141
   letter from, **148**
   in Newport, 64
   in New York, 111
   personality of, 35–36, 37, 43
   and World War I, 119, 123, **127**

Big Bertha (German gun), 129

Bourget, Minnie, 52, 53, **54**, 55, 63, 89, 133

Bourget, Paul, **54**
   and *Book of the Homeless*, 124
   and Pavillon Colombe, 133
   and social life, 66, 83, 87, 89, 90
   travels with, 63
   visits with, 52–54, 55

Brownell, William, 65

Burlingame, Edward L., 49, 54, 56, 79–80

Cavalry Episcopal Church, New York, 17

Century Magazine, 74

Chanler, Daisy, **142**

Children of Flanders Rescue Committee, 122–23, **124**

Codman, Ogden, **56**, 109, 110, 149
    and *The Decoration of Houses*, 58, 60, **60**, 66
    and Land's End, 50, 51, 56
    and The Mount, 65, 69, 71
    and Teddy, 51, 74

Cook, Charles:
    as chauffeur, 78–79, **78**, 83–84, 88, 91, 98, **115**, 123
    heart attack of, 150

D. Appleton, 107, 112

Darwin, Charles, *On the Origin of Species*, 43

Doyle, Hannah "Doyley," 2, 3, 4, 9, 18

Ehninger, John Whitten, portraits by, **3**, **5**

Eliot, T. S., 137

Europe:
    Aegean cruise, 139
    dancing lessons in, 7–8
    Edith's home in Paris, 89, **90**, 96, 100, 104, 105, 114, 134
    Edith's travels to, 29–30, 44–45, 55, 56, 63, 64, 75–78, 82–87, 88–91, **89**, 92, 94, 95, 98–99, 111–12, 139, 141, **142**
    Franco-Prussian War in, 8
    Jones family in, 4, 7–9, 25, 55–56
    Mediterranean cruises, 47–48, **142**
    Pavillon Colombe, outside Paris, 129–30, 133–34, **135**, 138, 149

Europe (*cont.*)
    St. Claire, Hyères, 132–34, **137**, 141, 149
    salons of Paris, 83, 87, 89–90, 91, 134
    World War I in, 113–30; *see also* World War I

Farrand, Beatrix Jones, 149
    early years of. *See* Jones, Beatrix

Fitzgerald, F. Scott, *The Great Gatsby*, 138

Fitz-James, Comtesse Robert de (Rosa):
    death of, 141
    Edith's friendship with, 89–90
    salons of, 83, 87, 89–90, 91, 134
    and the war, 134

Flagg, James Montgomery, poster by, **128**

Four Hundred, 46, 49–50, 53

Foxy (puppy), 3, 9

Franco-Prussian War, 8

French Legion of Honor, Edith as Chevalier of, 126

French Lick Resort, **106**

French Red Cross, 116, 119

Fullerton, William Morton, **97**
    Edith's relationship with, 92, 93–95, 96, 98–99, 100, 106, 139, 141
    and Edith's writing, 91, 107, 145
    and Love Diary, 92, 151–52
    in Paris, 91, 96
    travels with, 93, 98
    and women, 96

Gilded Age, 41, 50, 103

Goethe, poetry of, 18

Grace Church, New York, 2, **22**

Great War. *See* World War I

Greek mythology, Edith's interest in, 8

Gross, Catherine, 41, 44, 72, 98, 150

Harper's, 110

Harrison, Benjamin, 37

Hassam, Childe, painting by, **15**

Homberg, Madame, **147**

Howells, William Dean, 23

Hugh-Smith, John, 96, 102, 108, 141, 146,
    147

James, Henry, **75**, **83**, 85, 88
    and automobiles, 76, 77, **78**, 83–84, 91
    and Edith's home in England, 116
    and Edith's writing, 66, 67–68, 70, 108
    home of, **76**, 77
    illness and death of, 125, 141
    personality of, 76
    socializing with, 76, 77, 87, 90–91, 95–
        96, 98, 102–3
    and World War I, 125
    writing life of, 90

Jones, Beatrix (Freddy's daughter), 10, 13,
    31, 39, 50, 55, 64, 70, 110, 149

Jones, Edith, **25**, **33**
    baptism of, 2
    birth of, 1, 2
    childhood of, 2–10, **4**, **9**, 13–17
    coming-out party for, 25–27
    drawing and painting, **19**
    early writings of. *See* Jones, Edith,
        writings of

Jones, Edith (*cont.*)
    engagement to Teddy, 38–40, **39**
    in Europe, 29–30
    and father's death, 30
    and Henry Stevens, 27–32, 38
    intelligence of, 7, 10, 13, 14, 19, 24, 32,
        36–37
    making up stories, 4–5, 9
    marriage to Teddy, 40–41; *see also*
        Wharton, Edith
    mock reviews written by, 21, **21**
    reading, 5–6, 9, 16, 18, 19, 25
    social life of, 27, 29, 34
    and society's expectations, 10,
        24–27
    teen years of, **16**, 17–23, **19**, 25, 29–30,
        29

Jones, Edith, writings of, 16–17, 36–37
    Fast and Loose, 11, 20–22
    translation, 22
    Verses, 22–23, **23**

Jones, Elizabeth (aunt), 3, 8

Jones, Freddy (brother):
    affairs of, 46, 50
    childhood of, 2, 3, **3**, 4
    death of, 141
    divorce of, 56, 58, 110
    and his mother's death, 70
    in Maine, 28, 34
    and marriage, 10, 110
    in Newport, 13
    in New York, 31
    in Paris, 56, 64
    teasing his sister, 19

Jones, George Frederic (father), 1–2, 3, **3**, 4, **5**, **30**, 110
    death of, 30–31
    and Edith's childhood, 5, 16
    health problems of, 25, 29, 30
    social life of, 18
Jones, Harry (brother), **25**
    at Cambridge University, 4
    childhood of, 2
    death of, 141
    and Edith's poems, 23
    friends of, 27, 37
    and his mother's death, 70
    in Maine, 34
    in Newport, 13
    in Paris, 55–56, 64
    teasing his sister, 19
    and women, 108–9, 110, 112
Jones, Joshua (distant relative), 48
Jones, Lucretia (mother), **6**, **25**, **39**, 110
    death of, 69–70
    and Edith's adolescence, 19–20
    and Edith's birth, 1–2
    and Edith's childhood, 5–7
    and Edith's poems, 22
    and Freddy's divorce, 56, 58
    and Henry Stevens, 30
    and her husband's death, 31
    and marriage for Edith, 37, 38
    New York home of, **57**
    in Paris, 56
    social life of, 18
    and society's rules, 7, 8, 9, 20, 24, 26, 27, 28

Jones, Minnie (Freddy's wife), 10, 39, 66, 145
    death of, 146
    divorce of, 56, 64, 70
    as Edith's friend, 13, 19, 99
    Edith's letters to, 104, 133
    and Edith's writing, 136
    and Freddy's affairs, 46, 50
    in Maine, 28, 34
    in New York, 31, 55, 64, 111
    and World War I, 120, 123, 128
Jones family:
    in Europe, 4, 7–9, 25, 55–56
    financial situation of, 25–26, 31, 48
    Newport home of, 3–4, 9–10, 13–15, **14**
    New York home of, 3, 9–10, 31, 55, **57**
Joyce, James, *Ulysses*, 136–37
Judge, **46**

Kingsley, Charles, *The Water-Babies*, 7
Kinnicutt, Francis, 97

Land's End, Newport, **50**, 51, 53, 56, 64, 66
Lapsley, Gaillard:
    Edith's friendship with, 85–86, 87, 90, 95, 102, 108, 110
    Edith's letters to, 104
    and St. Claire Christmas Club, 133, 146, **147**
Lenox, Massachusetts:
    household staff in, 72, 78

Lenox, Massachusetts (*cont.*)
    The Mount in, **65**, 66, 68, **68**, 69, 71–
        73, **71**, 75, **75**, 77, 79, 88, **93**, 95,
        104, **105**
    residence in, 64–65
Lewis, Sinclair, 138
Lippincott's Magazine, 66
Longfellow, Henry Wadsworth, 23
Lubbock, Percy:
    Edith's friendship with, 85–86, 87, 90,
        108, 110
    travels with, 112
    and World War I, 119, 120
Ludendorff, Erich, 130

MacDonald, George, *The Princess and the
    Goblin,* 7
Mariano, Nicky, 144
Mason, Mary, 15
McAllister, Ward, 12, **12**, 25, 38, **46**, 134
    and the Four Hundred, 46, 49, 53
McClellen, Katherine, portrait by, **83**
Meyer, George, 74
Michelet, Mademoiselle, 7–8
Morton, Mrs. Levi, 26
Mount, The. *See* Lenox, Massachusetts
Mount Athos, Greece, 47

Newport, Rhode Island:
    country walks in, 14–15
    and Edith's health, 60, 64
    Land's End in, **50**, 51, 53, 56, 64, 66
    lawn tennis in, **28**
    Pencraig Cottage in, 13, 41, **42**, 48

Newport, Rhode Island (*cont.*)
    Pencraig in, 13–15, **14**, 31
    social life in, 27, 43, 45–46, 136
New York City:
    Academy of Music, **26**, 38, 46
    Delmonico's Restaurant in, 26, 34
    family life in, 18
    Fifth Avenue, 15–16, **15**
    the Four Hundred in, 46, 49–50, 53
    Jones family in, 3, 9–10, 31, 55, **57**
    Metropolitan Opera House in, 38, 46
    "nobs" and "swells" in, 11
    Old Guard in, 11–12, 28, 34, 38, 46, 50
    Patriarchs' Balls in, 25, 34, 38
    Patriarchs in, 12
    society's rules in, 16–17, 24–27, 28, 38,
        39–40, 46, 48, 49, 99, 111, 134,
        135–36, 152
    Whartons' homes in, 48, 50–51, **57**
New York Times, 49
North American Review, 23
Norton, Charles Eliot, 72, 87
Norton, Lily, 73
Norton, Robert, 96, 132, 133, 146, **147**
    painting of St. Claire by, **137**
Norton, Sally:
    death of, 141
    Edith's friendship with, 72, 74, 80, 87,
        99
    Edith's letters to, 75, 82, 89, 116, 117,
        118
    and Morton Fullerton, 91

Old Guard, 11–12, 28, 34, 38, 46, 50

Patriarchs, 12
Pavillon Colombe (outside Paris), 129–30,
    133–34, **135**, 139, 149
Pencraig, Newport, 13–15, **14**, 31
Pencraig Cottage, Newport, 13, 41, **42**, 48
Powel, Peter, portrait by, **102**
Pulitzer Prize, 136, 138

Rhinelander, Grandmother, 7
Rice, Allen Thorndike, 23
Rutherford, Lewis, 13–14
Rutherford, Louisa, 14, 28, 29
Rutherford, Margaret, 14, 28
Rutherford, Winthrop, 14, 18

St. Claire, Hyères, 132–34, **137**, 141, 149
St. Claire Christmas Club, 134, 146, **147**
Sarajevo, Austrian archduke assassinated
    in, 113–14
Scribner's: Charles Scribner's Sons, 49,
    54, 59, 61, 65, 79–80, 107, 112, 138
Scribner's Magazine:
    Edith's poems published in, 48–49
    Edith's short stories and articles in,
        54–55, 60, 110
    Edith's wartime writings for, 116, 119,
        120, 123
    House of Mirth serialized in, 79–80
Sloane, Emily Vanderbilt (Mrs. William),
    68, 69, 72
Stevens, Henry "Harry," 27–32, 38
    death of, 43
    in Europe, 30
    gossip about Edith and, 28, 31–32, 43

Stevens, Henry "Harry," (*cont.*)
    parents of, 27–28
Stevens, Mrs. Paran, 27, 31–32, 38
Stewart, Alexander, 12
Sturgis, Howard, **75**, 91, 103
    death of, 141
    Edith's friendship with, 87, 90, 95
    home of, 84–85, **84**, **86**
    personality of, 85

Tennyson, Alfred, Lord, 7
Twain, Mark, 41
Tyler, Bill, 121, 122, 127, 135, 147, 149
Tyler, Elisina, **122**, 139, 151
    and Edith's health, 141, 145, 149, 150
    war work of, 120–22, 128

Vanadis cruise, 47
Van Alen, James, 47, 48
Vanderbilt family, 49–50, 88

Washburn, Edward, 17, 18, 22, 30, 31
Washburn, Emelyn, 17–18, 30, 31
    and Edith's writing, 21, 22
    eye problems of, 39
Wharton, Billy, 37, 101
Wharton, Edith, **45**, **80**, **82**, **102**, **136**, **144**,
    147
    aging, 145–47, 149
    and automobiles, 76–78, **78**, 91, 98,
        115
    awards and honors to, 126, 136, 138,
        138
    death of, 149–50

Wharton, Edith, (*cont.*)

and divorce, 103–4, 105–6, 109–10, 111, 112

and dogs, 41–42, 44, **59**, 61, 88, 89, 146, 147, **153**

early years of, *see* Jones, Edith

finances of, 41, 48, 139

and French Legion of Honor, 126

grave of, 150

and her husband, *see* Wharton, Edward "Teddy"

and her mother's death, 69–70

household staff of, 72, 78, 150

intellectual friends of, 43–44, 72, 83–87, 95, 102, 108

journal of, 47, 71, 92, 94, 141, 151–52

and Mediterranean cruises, 47–48, **142**

in Newport, *see* Newport

personality of, 63

posthumous discoveries about, 151–52

Pulitzer Prize to, 136, 138

reading, 43–45, 53–54

and scientific rationalism, 143–44

and social life, 46–47, 99, 152

in wartime. *See* World War I

writing life of, 61–63, 65, 79, 149

writings of. *See* Wharton, Edith, writings of

Wharton, Edith, writings of, 171–72

The Age of Innocence, 134–36, 138, **140**, 151

"All Souls," 146

"Atrophy," 88

Wharton, Edith, writings of (*cont.*)

autobiography (*A Backward Glance*), 61, 74, 145

The Book of the Homeless, 124–25

The Buccaneers, 146

Certain People, 145

The Children, 142

"Copy," 94

Crucial Instances, 69

The Custom of the Country, 110, 126

The Decoration of Houses, 56, 58–59, 60, **60**, 66

Ethan Frome, 104–5, **108**, 126

film adaptations of, 172–73

The Fruit of the Tree, 24

"The Fulness of Life," 54–55

The Gods Arrive, 145

The Greater Inclination, 61, 63

The House of Mirth, 35, 79–82, **81**, 83, 87, 91

Hudson River Bracketed, 145

income from, 139

"The Introducers," 52

Italian Villas and Their Gardens, 74

"Kerfol," 131

"The Last Giustiniani," 49

"The Line of Least Resistance," 66, 67, 68–69

Literature, 112, 123–24, 126

magazine articles, 55

The Marne, 113, 134

"Mrs. Manstey's View," 49

"The Pelican," 60

poetry, 48–49

Wharton, Edith, writings of (*cont.*)

   The Reef, 106, 107, 108

   Sanctuary, 75

   serializations of, 79–80, 91

   short stories, 49, 54–55, 56, 60, 61, 63,
      65–66, 69, 110

   A Son at the Front, 134

   Summer, 126

   "Terminus," 98

   Twilight Sleep, 101, 144

   "The Valley of Childish Things, and
      Other Emblems," 1

   The Valley of Decision, 65, 67, 70, 76,
      86

   Walter Berry's help and support for,
      58–59, 60–61, 67, 82, 107, 136,
      142

   in wartime, 115–16, 119, 120, 123

   The World Over, 146

   The Writing of Fiction, 137–38

Wharton, Edward "Teddy," 37–42

   affairs of, 100

   and automobiles, 76–78, **78**, 83

   and companionship, 41, 63, 73, 88,
      143, 149

   death of, 142–43

   and dogs, **62, 73**

   Edith's engagement to, 38–40, **39**

   in Europe, 44–45, 55, 56, 76–78, 88,
      100, 105–6

   and father's illness, 38, 40, 69

   marriage of Edith and, 40–41, 105–7,
      109–10

   on Mediterranean cruise, 47–48

Wharton, Edward "Teddy," (*cont.*)

   mental health problems of, 73–74, 75,
      92–93, 95, 96–98, 101–4, 142, 143

   and money, 48, 70, 100, 104

   and The Mount, 69, 71–73, **73**, 75, **75**

   in Newport, 42

Wharton, Nannie, 38, 64, 97, 100, 101,
   109, 142

White, Alfred, 48, 72, 105, 111, 150

Wilson, Woodrow, 128

Winthrop, Egerton, 43–44, 48, 50, 53–54,
   87, 90, 141, 143

Woolf, Virginia, 137

World War I, 113–30

   American Hostels for Refugees, 120,
      121, **121**

   armistice, 130

   Big Bertha (German gun), 129

   Children of Flanders Rescue Commit-
      tee, 122–23, **124**

   destruction of, 131–32, 134

   Edith in England during, 116–17

   Edith in France during, 117–23, 128

   Edith's fundraising in, 119–20, 124–
      26, 127

   Edith's magazine articles to U.S. from,
      115–16, 119, 120, 123

   Edith's visits to battlefields in, **127**,
      129

   Edith's workroom organized in, 116–
      17, 118–19, **118**, 120, 126

   Edith's writing to support her charities
      in, 124–25

   end of, 130, 131–32

World War I (*cont.*)

    in France, 114–15, 116–17, 119–23,
        126–30

    as Great War, 132, 134

    impact of, 134

    onset of, 113–14

    Paris peace talks, 132

World War I (*cont.*)

    refugees in, 119–20

    and Tyler, 120–22, 128

    U.S. entry into, 123, 128–29, **128**

Yale University, honorary degree from,
    138, **138**